PROBLEMS OF THE MODERN ECONOMY

Labor and the National Economy

PROBLEMS OF THE MODERN ECONOMY

General Editor: EDMUND S. PHELPS, *Columbia University*

Each volume in this series presents
prominent positions in the debate of
an important issue of economic policy

———————————————————

AGRICULTURAL POLICY IN AN AFFLUENT SOCIETY

THE BATTLE AGAINST UNEMPLOYMENT

CHANGING PATTERNS IN FOREIGN TRADE
  AND PAYMENTS

THE CRISIS OF THE REGULATORY COMMISSIONS

DEFENSE, SCIENCE, AND PUBLIC POLICY

THE GOAL OF ECONOMIC GROWTH

INEQUALITY AND POVERTY

LABOR AND THE NATIONAL ECONOMY

MONOPOLY POWER AND ECONOMIC PERFORMANCE

POLLUTION, RESOURCES, AND THE ENVIRONMENT

PRIVATE WANTS AND PUBLIC NEEDS

THE UNITED STATES AND THE DEVELOPING ECONOMIES

THE URBAN ECONOMY

Labor
and the
National Economy

Edited with an introduction by

WILLIAM G. BOWEN

PRINCETON UNIVERSITY

and

ORLEY ASHENFELTER

PRINCETON UNIVERSITY

REVISED EDITION

NEW YORK
W · W · NORTON & COMPANY · INC ·

Copyright © 1975, 1965 by W. W. Norton & Company, Inc.

Library of Congress Cataloging in Publication Data
Bowen, William G   ed.
  Labor and the national economy

  (Problems of the modern economy)
  Bibliography: p.
  1. Labor economics—Addresses, essays, lectures. 2. Trade-unions—United
States—Addresses, essays, lectures. 3. Minorities—Employment—United
States—Addresses, essays, lectures. 4. Inflation (Finance)—United States—
Addresses, essays, lectures. I. Ashenfelter, Orley, 1942–   II. Title.
HD8072.B693   1975   331′.0973   75–23304
ISBN 0–393–05456–X
ISBN 0–393–09996–2 pbk.

Published simultaneously in Canada
by George J. McLeod Limited, Toronto

The Current Profile of the Labor Movement, from *Labor and the American Community*
by Derek Bok and John Dunlop (Simon and Schuster, 1970). Copyright 1970 by
The Rockefeller Brothers Fund, Inc. Reprinted by permission of The Rockefeller
Brothers Fund, Inc.
Labor Unions and Economic Policy, by Milton Friedman: from "Some Comments on
the Significance of Labor Unions for Economic Policy," in *The Impact of the Union*,
edited by David McCord Wright (Harcourt, Brace & World, 1951).
Labor and Antitrust, by Arthur J. Goldberg: from *I.U.D. Digest* (AFL–CIO), Winter
1958.
The Economics of Minimum-wage Legislation, by George J. Stigler: from *American
Economic Review*, June 1946. Copyright 1946 by the American Economic Association.
Minimum-wage Legislation: Another View, by Fred H. Blum: from *American Economic
Review*, September 1947. Copyright 1947 by the American Economic Association.
On Improving the Economic Status of the Negro, by James Tobin: from *Daedalus*,
Fall 1965. Copyright 1965 by The American Academy of Arts and Sciences. Reprinted
by permission of *Daedalus*, Journal of The American Academy of Arts and Sciences.
An Economic and Social Profile of the Negro American, by Rashi Fein: from *Daedalus*,
Fall 1965. Copyright 1965 by The American Academy of Arts and Sciences. Re-
printed by permission of *Daedalus*, Journal of The American Academy of Arts and
Sciences.
Capitalism and Discrimination, from *Capitalism and Freedom* by Milton Friedman.
Copyright 1962 by the University of Chicago Press. Reprinted by permission of the
University of Chicago Press.
The Economic Role of Women, by Barbara R. Bergmann and Irma Adelman: from
American Economic Review, March 1973. Copyright 1973 by the American Economic
Association.
What Price Guideposts? by Milton Friedman: from *Guidelines, Informal Controls and
the Market Place*, edited by George P. Shultz and Robert Z. Aliber. Copyright 1966 by
the University of Chicago Press. Reprinted by permission of the University of
Chicago Press.
The Case Against the Case Against the Guideposts, by Robert M. Solow: from
Guidelines, Informal Controls and the Market Place, edited by George P. Schultz
and Robert Z. Aliber. Copyright 1966 by the University of Chicago Press. Reprinted
by permission of the University of Chicago Press.

PRINTED IN THE UNITED STATES OF AMERICA

1 2 3 4 5 6 7 8 9

Contents

Introduction vii

PART ONE: The Setting 1
DEREK BOK and JOHN DUNLOP · The Current Profile of the Labor Movement 1

WILLIAM S. PEIRCE and RONALD L. OAXACA · The United States Labor Force 22

PART TWO: Efficiency Issues 30
MILTON FRIEDMAN · Labor Unions and Economic Policy 30

ARTHUR J. GOLDBERG · Labor and Antitrust 43

GEORGE J. STIGLER · The Economics of Minimum-wage Legislation 49

FRED H. BLUM · Minimum-wage Legislation: Another View 57

PART THREE: Labor Problems of Minorities and Women 63
JAMES TOBIN · On Improving the Economic Status of the Negro 63

RASHI FEIN · An Economic and Social Profile of the Negro American 83

MILTON FRIEDMAN · Capitalism and Discrimination 106

COUNCIL OF ECONOMIC ADVISERS · The Economic Role of Women 116

BARBARA R. BERGMANN and IRMA ADELMAN · The Economic Role of Women: An Appraisal 145

PART FOUR: Inflation and Unemployment 153
WILLIAM G. BOWEN and RONALD L. OAXACA · Wage Behavior and the Cost-Inflation Problem 153

COUNCIL OF ECONOMIC ADVISERS · Noninflationary Wage and Price Behavior 163

MILTON FRIEDMAN · What Price Guideposts? 170

ROBERT M. SOLOW · The Case Against the Case Against the Guideposts 190

Suggested Further Readings 205

E 24543 G.

Introduction

IN THE LAST TWENTY YEARS the general public, government officials, and professional economists have become increasingly aware of the extent to which the success of our economic system depends on the workings of labor markets. Policy-making groups such as the President's Council of Economic Advisers have found themselves devoting considerably more attention to such things as the outcome of wage negotiations in basic industries, the implications of dramatic shifts in the composition of the labor force (white-collar workers, roughly 18 percent of the labor force in 1900, now comprise close to 50 percent), and the effects of minimum-wage laws, overtime provisions, and other labor legislation on the health of the economy. "Labor monopoly," "cost inflation," and "racial discrimination"—these are some of the phrases used to describe key policy issues, and no one who reads a daily newspaper needs to be told that they describe an exciting, controversial, and often murky area.

An appreciation of the broad sweep of labor-market developments is necessary for an understanding of the pros and cons of these substantive policy issues. The two essays in Part One are intended to satisfy this requirement. In the first essay, excerpted from *Labor and the American Community*, Derek Bok and John Dunlop describe the labor movement in the United States, looking closely at the average union member and examining the issues of power and politics in the functioning of unions.

The other essay in Part One examines the major trends in the labor market in this century—the marked increase of married women in the labor force, the trend toward lower labor force rates among the aged, and the decline in the importance of manual labor.

Parts Two, Three, and Four reflect the diverse ways in which events in the labor market affect issues of general economic policy. The essays in Part Two debate the effects of unionization and other characteristics of contemporary labor markets on the efficiency with which the economy allocates its resources and on the distribution of income. The special labor-market problems of minority-group members and women, areas of great social importance and current concern, are examined in Part Three. Part Four focuses on the interrelated macroeconomic problems of inflation and unemployment.

EFFICIENCY AND INCOME DISTRIBUTION

Milton Friedman opens Part Two with a lively and controversial article on the effects of unions on relative wages and thus on the allocative efficiency of the economy. He argues that "laymen and economists alike tend . . . to exaggerate greatly the extent to which labor unions affect the structure and level of wage rates." But this is not to say that unions have no effect. Friedman contends that the similarities between labor monopoly and enterprise monopoly should be emphasized and that, from a policy standpoint, "it is highly important to have labor monopoly covered by the Sherman Antitrust Act." In the second article, Arthur J. Goldberg, formerly an Associate Justice of the Supreme Court, takes the opposite view. Putting unions under federal antitrust laws, he argues, would so weaken them that they would no longer be able to perform their socially desirable functions. He also asserts that, historically, the alternative to unionism has not been "real competition" in the labor market but monopoly power on the side of the employers.

This pair of essays, which debate the economic power of unions, is in the historical mainstream of labor-market analysis. Labor unions do constitute a special form of economic organization, and the traditional emphasis in policy discussions on evaluating the economic—as well as the social and political—effects of unionization is easily understood. It is well to remember, however, that only about one-fourth of our working population belongs to unions, and that even in the unionized sectors considerations besides union strength—the economic environment, management policies, government legislation, and worker mobility—influence wages and working conditions.

Minimum-wage laws are an important instance of substantive government intervention in labor markets; the economic effects of such legislation are debated by George Stigler and Fred Blum in the next two essays. Although the federal minimum wage has been raised several times since these essays were written, the fundamental issues remain much the same. Indeed, Stigler's charge that minimum-wage legislation is not an effective way to combat poverty is, if anything, more topical now, in the context of current antipoverty programs. Blum answers this charge by emphasizing the specialized objectives of minimum-wage legislation and the importance of appraising its effects in terms of the workings of the imperfect labor and product markets of the real world.

LABOR PROBLEMS OF MINORITIES AND WOMEN

Countering criticis like J. K. Galbraith and Michael Harrington, who believe that modern economic progress has "left behind" segments of American society, James Tobin opens Part Three with a plea for a healthy economy as the best cure for the problems of the disadvantaged. Maintaining a tight labor market through national fiscal and monetary policy, increasing the fight against discrimination through stricter enforcement of current fair-employment laws, and establishing a fair and incentives-maintaining way of supporting the earning capacity of people unable to do it themselves are the three parts of Tobin's plan to improve the economic status of minority groups.

In the second article, Rashi Fein presents a detailed description of the socioeconomic state of American blacks, both in comparison with white America today and in terms of the progress, or lack of it, seen in this century. He finds that, while great absolute strides have been made, the gains in such crucial areas as health, education, and income are negligible when compared to the advances of the society as a whole. Pointing to the interrelatedness of these areas and the evidence of discrimination, Fein calls for acceptance of preferential social policy to close the socioeconomic gap between blacks and whites.

The conclusions of the next article by Milton Friedman contrast sharply with Fein's arguments. Discrimination, according to Friedman, is simply another taste represented in the market, similar analytically to other preferences. While he deplores the practice of racial inequality, he concludes that restrictions placed upon the market, such as fair-employment-practices legislation, are the wrong corrective actions to use. He advocates instead a greater dependence upon the market system in areas where it is not now used, such as education, coupled with an expression of antidiscrimination sentiments through that system. His proposal for educational vouchers, advanced over a decade ago, has begun to receive unexpected support among parents in urban areas and elsewhere.

The fourth article originally appeared as Chapter 4 in the 1973 Report of the President's Council of Economic Advisers and takes up the special role and problems of women in the labor market. This article provides a detailed summary of labor force, unemployment, and earnings statistics of women and contrasts them with the comparable figures for men, concluding that it is difficult to evaluate the extent to which women's capabilities have actually been underutilized by society when all factors are considered. The next article, by Barbara Bergmann and Irma Adelman, was written specifically as a survey and critique of the preceding selection. Though they emphasize the sources of their agreement, Bergmann and Adelman are especially critical of the "sociological conservation" they feel is embedded in Council's statement and the failure of the Council to propose concrete programs of government action to remedy the special labor-market problems of women.

INFLATION AND UNEMPLOYMENT

In recent years, the macroeconomic problems of inflation, un-employment, and growth have continued to receive more atten-tion from policy-makers than the microeconomic problems of allocation and distribution. To this generalization can be added another: It is now recognized, to a much greater extent than be-fore, that monetary and fiscal policies alone may not suffice to satisfy the national goal of high employment and reasonable price stability; "active" labor-market policies may also be re-quired.

"Cost inflation" is a phrase born of the concern that wage settlements between powerful contending parties—large unions and industries dominated by large firms—were forcing a type of persistent inflation on the country which could not be dealt with successfully by orthodox monetary and fiscal policies. William Bowen and Ronald Oaxaca's essay attempts to clarify the conceptual basis of the cost-inflation controversy and to present empirical evidence that can be used to judge the seriousness of the problem. The relationship between the rate of change of wages, the rate of change of productivity, and the level of unemployment is stressed, since this relationship is an important determinant of the compatibility of price stability and high employment. If money wages rise more rapidly than productivity (that is, if unit labor costs rise), the formulators of monetary and fiscal policy are faced with an unpleasant choice: Increasing aggregate demand will in all likelihood lead to still greater increases in unit labor costs and additional upward pressure on the price level, while decreasing demand will lead to still more unemployment. In the period 1948–1972 unit labor costs tended to rise even when unemployment was 6 percent or lower.

Many policies for dealing with cost inflation have been suggested, but the history of economic policy over the last decade regarding this issue seems to have repeated itself. An important point of departure in this history was the description of "noninflationary wage and price behavior" set forth by the Kennedy Administration's Council of Economic Advisers in the January 1962 Economic Report of the President, which we have included here in full. This description was a prelude to the now famous wage and price guidepost policy of 1962–1966, which was abandoned only after the protracted inflationary period surrounding the Vietnamese conflict had erupted. Upon taking office in early 1969 the Nixon Administration initially renounced any efforts toward wage or price policies along the lines that had been followed in 1962–1966, but in the fall of 1971 it reversed this position fully with the adoption of a "new economic policy" that included an interim wage and price freeze followed by an elaborate set of wage and price guidelines. Although written in the context of the controversy surrounding the Kennedy Administration's guidepost policy, the arguments of the next two essays in Part Four are a nearly perfect reflection of the debate that surrounded the Nixon Administration's new economic policy. Subsequently, the Nixon and Ford Administrations have retreated from the guideline policies, but debate continues over the role that the federal government should play in wage and price policies and these essays continue to capture the essence of that discussion.

Milton Friedman views wage and price controls as ineffective because they are not directed toward the true cause of inflation, a rapidly rising money supply. In fact, Friedman emphasizes, controls are not only ineffective but harmful because inflation while supposedly suppressed is only concealed and therefore far more dangerous. Robert Solow, however, in the companion article on this issue, presses the case for wage-price guideposts, noting that while certainly not the perfect instrument for controlling inflation, the guideposts are the best of the policies available. Solow reasons that because our current economic system is not a perfectly competitive one there is room for discretion in decision-making not motivated by market forces alone. Guideposts are helpful in channeling this discretionary action into activities retarding inflation and therefore are, according to Solow, a worthwhile national policy.

O. A. and W. B.

April 1975

PROBLEMS OF THE MODERN ECONOMY

Labor and the National Economy

PART ONE

The Setting

The Current Profile of the Labor Movement

DEREK BOK AND JOHN DUNLOP

Derek Bok is President of Harvard University and John Dunlop is Secretary of Labor. This essay is from their book Labor and the American Community.

IN 1966, 18.3 million men and women in the United States were paying dues to labor unions. By 1968, the figure is estimated to have exceeded 19 million. The number of employees subject to collective-bargaining agreements is still larger by three-quarters of a million, since not all employees covered by collective-bargaining agreements are required to be union members. The past five years have been a period of marked expansion in the total number of union members, reversing a decline which set in with the recession of 1958. Nevertheless, the labor force has grown so rapidly that union membership in 1968, as a percentage of employment in nonagricultural enterprises, was little more than 28 percent compared to the level of 33–34 percent achieved in the middle 1950s.

Union members are organized into more than 70,000 local unions, which are in turn affiliated with 190 national or international unions (except for fewer than a thousand locals, with an aggregate of little more than a half million members, that are directly affiliated with the AFL–CIO or in single-firm and local unaffiliated unions). Two-thirds of these national unions with more than three-quarters of the membership are affiliated with the AFL–CIO, even after the disaffiliation of Walter Reuther and the Auto Workers in 1968.

THE UNION MEMBER

Union members do not represent a mirror image of the entire adult population, or even the work force, of this country. Instead they are rather heavily concentrated in certain income ranges, educational levels, industries, occupations and regions.

Income · Unionists fall mainly in the middle-income group, with relatively few members numbered among the very rich or the very poor. In 1965, 69.1 percent of union heads of households had incomes ranging from $5,000 to $10,000. Among households headed by nonmembers, only 43.4 percent fell within this income range. Conversely, only 3.9 percent of union household heads received less than $3,000 during the same year, while 14.2 percent earned more than $10,000. For nonunion households, the corresponding figures were substantially larger; 14.3 percent fell below $3,000, while 21.6 percent earned over 10,000.

Education · Much the same pattern carries over to the area of education. In 1965, 44 percent of all union heads of households had an education that extended through all or part of high school (but not beyond). Only 32 percent of nonunion household heads fell within these categories. At the upper end of the scale, however, the figures were sharply reversed. Only 1.4 percent of all union family heads had received a college diploma and 0.4 percent had received an advanced degree. Among family heads who were not members of unions, over eight times as many (11.4 percent) had graduated from college, while almost twenty times as many (7.8 percent) had obtained an advanced degree.

Sex · It is well known that women workers are underrepresented in labor unions. Among employees outside the agricultural sector, only one woman in seven belongs to a union, while one man in every three is a member. To some extent, the difference is explained by the heavy employment of women in clerical and sales occupations and in service industries, where unions have traditionally made little headway. . . .

Industry and Occupation · Union members are distributed most unevenly among different industries, as the following table reveals:

Industry	Percentage organized
Transportation, communications, public utlilities	74.7%
Construction	70.9
Manufacturing	50.0
Mining	47.2
Government	14.1
Services	10.5
Trade	9.3
Finance, real estate	2.0
Agriculture	0.8

These differences are the result of many factors. The variations in the occupational mix of different industries are significant, for unions seem to have much greater appeal in some occupational groups than others. The prevalence of women in certain occupations helps to explain the low rate of unionization in the trade and service sectors. With a few notable exceptions, white-collar workers have traditionally been cool to unions, especially professional and technical employees. On the other hand, blue-collar employees in the skilled and semiskilled categories seem to be the most promising target for unionization. Unskilled laborers tend to fall between these poles. They are usually more susceptible than white-collar workers, but they are also more apt to be foreign-born, easily replaceable, quickly intimidated by hostile employers, subject to considerable turnover, and thus often frustrating to union organizers seeking to attract continuing affiliation. These differences reveal themselves dramatically in figures comparing the rates of unionization among occupations.

Occupations	Percentage organized
Operatives (semiskilled)	63%
Craftsmen and foremen	50
Laborers (excluding agriculture)	38
Clerical	26
Service	20
Sales	
Managers	} 5–10
Professional and technical	

Geography · Union membership is not distributed throughout in the United States in proportion to population or employment. In general terms, the extent of union organization—measured as a fraction of nonagricultural employment–is greatest in the east-north-central and eastern industrial states and on the West Coast. The extent of organization is least in the South, the Southwest and the Middle West plain states. There are, of course, important variations within these groupings. For example, there appears to be some tendency for employees in metropolitan areas to be slightly more highly organized than employees in smaller communities.

The five states with the largest employment—New York, California, Pennsylvania, Illinois, and Ohio—contain 48 percent of the union members while they employ 38 percent of the nonagricultural work force. These five states have 8.7 million union members.

Many more characteristics of union members could be cited. For example, it is interesting to note that the union movement includes about the same proportion of nonwhites as in the nonagricultural work force and that unions contain a disproportionate number of war veterans and Catholics. But even more important than these demographic factors are the attitudes of union employees on social, political, and economic questions. For, in the last analysis, these sentiments will probably have the most direct effects upon the course of union behavior.

The opinions of union members are particularly striking in their lack of any special class bias. This remarkable state of affairs has been commented upon by a number of European critics.

In the experience of the European, industrial strife was a conflict between two classes, almost two distinct orders of mankind, separated from each other by a wide and impossible gulf of habits, attitudes and material conditions. The European was fascinated (in the United States) by the general air of prosperity, the free-and-easy relations between persons on different social levels, the lack of social distinctions, class hostilities, class jealousies, class political issues.

Today, the same pattern still reveals itself in opinion surveys on a wide variety of questions. Whether the issue is Vietnam, admission of Red China to the U.N., civil-rights legislation, aid to education, the poverty program, a labor party, or government ownership of essential industries, the opinions of union members come within a very few percentage points of those held by the public at large. The same is true of questions touching on attitudes toward society and government. Union members are no more likely than the general public is to feel, in the language of the interview question, that "the people running the country don't really care what happens to people like yourself." Nor are they more likely to feel that what they think "doesn't count very much" or to fear that they "don't have as good a chance to get ahead as most people." And they are as overwhelmingly disposed as the rest of society is to reject the notion that "nobody understands our problems" or that they are "left out of the things going on around us."

It is well to compare these findings with the standard theories that popular writers have expressed about the political sentiments of union members. One view, less prevalent now than two decades ago, maintains that union members are, more than the rest of the population, willing to support sweeping social and economic programs. Another theory has flowered more recently in the wake of repeated claims of "white backlash" in heavily blue-collar areas. According to this opinion, union members were more "progressive" in earlier decades but have become strongly conservative as their wages and conditions have risen to more comfortable middle-class levels.

Neither of these theories is well supported by the facts. According to recent opinion surveys, union members as a group do not exhibit any special desire for drastic social and economic change. They reject, by about the same margin as the general public, such current proposals as a negative income tax and a multibillion-dollar program for the cities. And they are much more anxious that the government finance the war in Vietnam and combat crime in the streets than that it maintain welfare programs and compaign against poverty. Nevertheless, union members are not more conservative about these matters than the rest of the population. If anything, they tend to stand two or three percentage points to the liberal side on matters of race, the United Nations, the poverty program, and most other public issues. These tendencies also seem to be remarkably durable. There has been no apparent shift to the right over the past two or three decades. On racial matters, for example, the attitudes of union members have grown steadily *more* tolerant, not less (along with those of most other segments of the society).

Various forces have contributed to this peculiar lack of class sentiment among union members (and other manual workers). One important factor was the extreme heterogeneity of the American labor force in the formative years of industrialization. During this period, a network of language, racial, and religious barriers was thrown up by repeated waves of immigration. Particular ethnic groups gained control over different jobs, while recent immigrants and Negro laborers were excluded from the better jobs and later used as strikebreakers by employers. These experiences produced cleavages that kept the labor movement from achieving the degree of unity reached in Great Britain and Scandinavia.

Labor organizations in America also grew up in a society that stressed the ideals of classlessness, individual initiative, and abundant opportunity, a society in which workers enjoyed the right of suffrage and the opportunity for a free public education. In this atmosphere, employees were less inclined than workers in Europe to submerge their sense of individuality and identify with a working class. Many of them, moreover, were constantly presented with opportunities to leave the ranks of labor for management jobs or opportunities in the West. In contrast to Europe, real wages were high and rose rapidly, and the spread between skilled and unskilled wage rates was especially large. As a result, class solidarity was slow to develop and potential leadership was constantly siphoned off into other pursuits.

In Europe, on the other hand, labor movements arose against the backdrop of a feudal tradition that denied workers access to economic opportunity or political power. Under these conditions, European workers were driven togther to make common cause to advance their interests. In the political sphere, for example, workers often had to struggle for a decade or more into the twentieth century to achieve such elementary rights as public education and, more important, universal male suffrage. As public issues, these questions were important enough to arouse the working classes for a sustained political effort. In contrast to the experience of America, where such rights were granted much earlier, in Europe ". . . the arising awareness of the working classes expressed above all an experience of *political alienation*— that is, a sense of not having a recognized position in the civic community or of not having a civic community in which to participate."

The sense of working-class solidarity, of separateness from the rest of society, still remains strong in countries like France and Italy. Elsewhere in Europe, notably in Scandinavia, manual workers seem gradually to have been integrated more closely into the entire population. Yet, traditions of working-class sentiment have left their mark upon the shape of the labor movement throughout the entire continent.

THE UNIONS

The American union movement has certain characteristics that give it a special flavor and set it somewhat apart from most of its counterparts abroad.

Size · Despite all of the concern expressed over labor's power, union membership in America is a smaller proportion of the work force than in any of the other major industrial democracies. While this fact is arresting in itself, its significance grows even larger when one realizes that higher levels of unionization have been achieved throughout Western Europe without benefit of the union shop, without elaborate legal safeguards to protect the workers' right to organize, and without expensive campaigns or professional staffs to organize nonunion employers.

The low levels of unionization in America can be explained largely by two factors. One important factor is the widespread opposition of employers—an attitude no longer prevalent in Europe save in Italy and France. Although American labor leaders often exaggerate the significance of this opposition, its importance can be seen in the ease with which unions can usually organize blue-collar workers once management has been persuaded to remain neutral. Employer opposition, however, does not wholly explain the stunted growth of the American labor movement. Unionization is proportionately much greater in Italy than in the United States despite widespread hostility from employers, and this has been true even though Italian unions have had to cope with severe internal divisions, less impressive achievements at the bargaining table, and an almost total lack of formal organizing efforts. In other countries, moreover, employers were often openly hostile toward unions in the early stages of organization, but their policies eventually changed because they could not overcome the determination of the unions.

A second factor has been the lack of solidarity among workers in the United States. Perhaps opportunities for advancement and geographic movement were greater in this country, thus strengthening the hold on individualism; perhaps employees were influenced by higher wages and rising living standards derived from a chronic scarcity of labor and rapidly increasing productivity. Whatever the explanation, the small size of the United States union movement must probably be attributed in part to the lack of a strongly felt need on the part of many employees to band together for mutual protection. In Europe, on the other hand, feelings of worker solidarity were much stronger. They were typically buttressed by a network of mutually reinforcing institutions based on working-class support—political parties, cooperatives, youth groups, educational programs, and even banks, newspapers, and other commercial undertakings. In short, though there is evidence in several countries that class lines may be weakening, the European labor leader has been able to capitalize on a cultural milieu in which union membership has been the natural response of the working man.

Unions and Politics · The lack of a distinctive ideology among the working people of this country has also had a marked influence on the political activity of American unions. The labor movement in the United States is unique in failing to produce a political party based explicitly on working-class support. Nor have American unions followed the example of many European countries by splitting into rival organizations based upon party lines. In France and in Italy, there are three large national organizations of workers representing Communist, Socialist, and Christian Democrat ideologies. In Belgium, Socialist and Christian Democrat federations coexist. In the Netherlands separate Catholic, Protestant, and Socialist labor organizations have been established. Cleavages have also developed in the United States, most notably during the thirties, when John L. Lewis and the Congress of Industrial Organizations defied the American Federation of Labor. But characteristically this division took place over pragmatic questions of tactics and jurisdiction in organizing the mass-production industries and not because of any deep-seated differences in religion or political philosophy. In keeping with the nature of the conflict, the differences between the AFL and CIO were submerged twenty years later in the formation of the AFL–CIO.

Strong Local Unions · Unions in this country were generally forced to achieve recognition and establish bargaining relationships on a plant-by-plant basis rather than by agreement with a strong national or regional association of employers. This process encouraged the growth of active local unions in the plant, with important functions to perform. In some industries, of course, control over collective bargaining has gravitated to the national or regional level. But even in these sectors, local unions still retain considerable influence over the administration of the contract and over political and community activities.

The importance of local unions is reflected in the financial holdings of labor organizations in the United States. At the end of 1966, all union bodies had combined assets of $1,839,000,000, and the combined assets of local unions and intermediate bodies exceeded those of the international unions. In the same year, local unions had receipts of $1,256,000,000, intermediate bodies net receipts of $14,000,000, and international unions net receipts of $560,000,000.

This pattern is not encountered abroad. Viable plant locals do exist in Scandinavia, but even there the grievance process is less developed than in this country, and local bodies have little or no control over political matters, organizing other plants, community activities, and similar matters that occupy the attention of many local unions in this country. In Britain and Australia, plant organizations may have a strong influence over local disputes and working conditions, but these bodies often behave quite independently of the national unions, to the frequent embarrassment of their parent organizations. On the continent of Europe, the contrast is even more marked. Local unions rarely exist at all and union representatives in the plant share whatever power they have over grievances and local problems with other institutions, such as the elected workers' councils, over which they have little direct control.

A Loose Federation · At higher levels in the union structure, the labor movement in America has remained markedly decentralized in the sense that the central federation has had relatively little authority over its member unions. In part, this is the result of the lack of a class sentiment strong enough to transcend the attachments of workers to their own separate crafts and occupations. In part, the absence of a strong federation reflected the predominance in our labor movement of bargaining rather than political action, for which a powerful central body would have been more necessary to enable the movement to act in unison in election campaigns and lobbying efforts. In any event, the AFL was founded with the explicit understanding that the affiliated unions would retain their autonomy. Throughout its history, the federation had to rely, with mixed success, on persuasion and conciliation instead of on exercising formal powers or sanctions. Even today the situation is not much changed. The AFL–CIO has acquired some power to investigate and suspend affiliates for corruption or Communist influence, but it has little or no authority over the bargaining and strike policies of its members, nor is it able to control their membership requirements or political activities.

There are other countries, notably Britain and Australia, where the central federation is also rather weak. But the situation is more often to the contrary. For example, the major Swedish federation negotiates directly with the central employers' organization to establish broad wage guidelines that are binding on its constituent unions. Member unions must also gain the consent of the federation before initiating a strike involving more than 3 percent of their membership and must agree to include various rules in their constitutions safeguarding the rights of individuals with respect to membership, discipline, transfers, and the like. Even in matters involving local grievances and discharges of workers, the federation has ultimate power to enter into binding settlements. In other European countries, the degree of power actually exercised by the central organizations is harder to assess, but certainly the Belgian and Dutch federations are highly centralized, and it is generally assumed that the dominant Communist federations in France and Italy have extensive control over the policies of their member unions.

THE NEAR UNIONS

It has been assumed that everyone understands what a union is in this country. But any careful newspaper reader will agree that the definition of "union" has become decidedly vague in recent years. A decade ago, the National Education Association, an organization of a million schoolteachers and administrators, prided itself on its status as a thoroughly professional association. Today, the teachers affiliated with N.E.A. have embraced the idea of negotiation with school boards and have resorted to strikes and other collective sanctions to achieve their proposals. Professional associations of nurses have come to engage in mass resignations and other forms of economic pressure to achieve collective agreements. In professional athletics, football, basketball, and baseball associations have all sprung up seeking negotiations and uttering ominous threats of stopping play. Police officers' associations in a few localities have invented the "blue plague," an exotic illness known only to uniformed patrolmen in search of improved benefits. And in Southern California an erstwhile man of the cloth has even tried to organize Catholic priests. The near unions tend to have supervisory employees as members; their members are more independent, have higher incomes, and are more responsive to professional concerns than are members of conventional unions. It is unclear whether these organizations are in transition toward more conventional unions or constitute a more permanent form of employee organization.

Although the total size of the near unions is uncertain, their combined membership is certainly greater than two million persons. With the addition of the near unions, the composition of membership in all employee organizations is less heavily concentrated than in the AFL–CIO alone among certain income and occupational groups. It is also more diverse in its goals, its strategies, and its political outlook.

THE UNION LEADER

In contrast to the labor movements in other countries, unions in the United States boast a much higher number of full-time officials. To some extent, this tendency may reflect a distinctive American attitude toward administration, for business enterprises, universities, and various other private organizations also seem to have particularly large staffs in this country. But the root of the matter, once again, lies in the decentralized pattern of union organization and labor relations in the United States. For the most part, collective bargaining has not consisted of negotiations with huge industrywide employer associations. The predominant tendency has been to conduct separate negotiations with individual plants and companies. As a result, there are a vast number of contracts to be negotiated. Because it is so decentralized, bargaining can also grapple with the particular working conditions of the individual plant to a degree not duplicated abroad. And once the agreement is signed, the local union is the natural agency for taking up the countless individual complaints and questions that arise concerning the application and administration of the contract. To perform all this work, a host of union officials is required.

Almost all labor leaders have come up from the ranks of the members working in the plants and crafts that the unions represent. Unlike the situation in several other countries, especially in the underdeveloped world, very few of these leaders have backgrounds as lawyers, politicians, editors, professors, or intellectuals. Nor are their fathers predominantly found outside the ranks of labor. In a 1967 survey of union presidents, secretary-treasurers, and vice-presidents, 37 percent were found to have fathers who were skilled workers; 17 percent were the sons of semiskilled and unskilled employees; 7 percent were the children of foremen. No more than 11 percent of the fathers owned a business and only 4 percent were executives.

At first glance, these figures seem surprising. In a mobile society without marked class divisions, one might have expected that union leaders would be drawn to a larger extent from different areas of society. But other forces have tugged more strongly in the opposite direction. Intellectuals and professionals are most often drawn to a labor movement as a vehicle for their own political advancement or a force for promoting certain political and social ideals. The American labor movement has been rather unattractive for these purposes, for it has never been profoundly ideological, nor has it provided a particularly easy entry to a political career. Instead, the work of the unions has centered upon the bargaining process and, especially at the lowest levels of the union hierarchy, upon the day-to-day business of administering the working conditions in the shop and factory. These issues require an intimate knowledge of the workplace naturally acquired by union members who have worked in the trade. To the intellectual or the professional man, however, these matters are not only unfamiliar; they are also of precious little interest.

Emerging as he does from the rank and file, the union leader naturally tends to reflect many of the characteristics of his membership. For example, 83 percent of union presidents and secretary-treasurers are said to be Democrats, just as almost all unions have a majority of Democrats among their members. As for education, approximately half of all union leaders in the 1967 survey have no more than a high-school education; while 21 percent have completed college, 25 percent never graduated from high school. The proportion of college graduates among union leaders is appreciably higher than among union members, but it lags well behind the level achieved by businessmen, government officials, and other key groups within the society.

The average age of the national officer of a union is fifty-three —about the same as for business executives at the vice-president and president level. According to the 1967 survey, the "typical" national officer is likely to have begun to work at roughly eighteen years of age. But he will probably not have become a union member until his early twenties and will not have joined his present union until three or four years later. Six or seven years after that he will have reached his first elective position in his union local. From local office, he will probably have taken an appointive staff position and then will have become a national officer at approximately age forty-five.

As one might expect, there are marked variations among officials and among unions. For example, union leaders tend to have higher levels of education if they belong to small unions or unions in the transportation, service, or government sectors. In most cases, these differences stem from variations in the type and background of the members in the various unions. Small elite crafts tend to be led by better-educated men. The Airline Pilots or Actors Equity will obviously produce a different kind of leader from that of the Mine Workers or the Laborers.

At one time, much was made of the differences between the leaders of CIO and AFL unions. According to the sociologist C. Wright Mills, "The AFL and CIO are not two differently shaped vessels filled with similar types of leaders. The split between them runs deep: It divides different types of men. They differ in their personal characterstics, in the union experience they have had, and in their social and political outlook." When Mills was writing, the CIO was little more than a decade old. Its young unions were filled with young leaders. Their education was frequently superior to that of the AFL leaders. To Mills, therefore, the AFL seemed largely a gerontocracy—". . . at its top are older men who are relatively poorly educated and who have authority over much younger men who are relatively better educated."

In the intervening years, these differences have all but disappeared. According to the 1967 survey, the average age of CIO leaders is fifty-three; for AFL leaders, fifty-six. The percentage of CIO leaders who have completed college is twelve; of AFL leaders, twenty-two. In sum, the divergent statistics that Mills developed were largely the accidents of history. They reflected the youth of the CIO and disappeared as soon as these unions increased in age. And as they disappeared, many of the differences in social and political outlook tended to diminish as well. . . .

THE DETERMINANTS OF UNION BEHAVIOR

. . . At present, most commentators seem to assume that the future of the labor movement rests mainly in the hands of its leaders. This point of view is reflected in the constant criticism of labor leaders, and it is buttressed by a mass of opinion data to the effect that unions are run pretty much as the top officials see fit. Yet one must beware of such opinions, for each of the groups that most influence the public view of organized labor has its special reasons for misconceiving the role of the union leader and exaggerating his influence.

The businessman, for example, is accustomed to organizations where the leader enjoys considerable power (though not so much as the outsider tends to suppose). As a result, many executives assume instinctively that the union leader enjoys comparable authority; they overlook the fact that union officials must win office by election. Businessmen may also exaggerate the role of the union leader as a result of their natural tendency to assume a "harmony of interests" between themselves and their employees. This assumption has suffused the literature of business for decades and stems, once again, from understandable motives. Few managements wish to harbor the thought that they are pursuing their own interests at the expense of their employees. It would be most disagreeable to concede that wages are kept unfairly low or that the quest for efficiency has led to harsh supervision or uncomfortable working conditions. As a result, when employees organize or protest or strike, many employers assume that harmonious relations within their plants have been disrupted by some opportunistic union leader who has succeeded in leading the workers astray. This reaction, once again, is not a simple matter of tactics; it springs naturally from a network of beliefs that help many executives to justify their behavior as businessmen and human beings.

Intellectuals also have their reasons for ascribing great influence to the union leader. As Bertrand Russell has pointed out, the liberal critic has traditionally been sentimental toward the underdog. He has been unable to champion the cause of the poor and the disadvantaged without idealizing them as well. As a result—until recently, at any rate—these critics could seldom bring themselves to blame union shortcomings on the members; instead, they concluded that the leaders must somehow be responsible.

Other forces also helped to reinforce the bias. After the rush of organizing in the thirties, union members seemed to have become representative of the entire working class. Under these circumstances, it would have been most awkward to fault the members for labor's failure to press for social reform. How could the liberal justify his programs if the beneficiaries themselves were indifferent to them? Unless the rank and file were on his side, how could he urge the unions to reform and still keep true to his democratic principles? Above all, how could be harbor any optimism at all if the entire working class had to be persuaded to support his programs? With all these difficulties, it was far easier to assume that unions were made up of willing members who were held back by the stubbornness and selfishness of powerful leaders. These beliefs could begin to weaken only when union members were no longer seen as representative of the lower classes and unions were no longer the only organized force for social reform. Thus, it is no accident that intellectuals did not acknowledge the lack of liberal, reformist sentiments among the members until the 1960s, when students, black militants, and other groups had already begun to offer organized support for fundamental social reforms. (Characteristically enough, now that the pendulum has begun to swing, it has swung very far indeed in the minds of many criticis. Union members are now viewed not only as apathetic and undisposed to social reform; they are erroneously perceived as a highly conservative force in the society.)

Because of these tendencies to exaggerate the influence of the labor leader, one must take pains to construct a more realistic picture of how union policy is actually made. Otherwise, society will often misdirect its energies by flailing away at union officials for actions that are not really within their power to change. In the process, deeper forces may be overlooked, forces that actually determine union behavior and must ultimately be changed if the conduct of unions is to change.

In the end, union behavior is the product of four broad influences that are constantly interacting upon one another: the desires of the members, the nature and abilities of the leadership, the capacities and opinions of subordinates, and the pressures of the environment. This has been a series of illustrations showing how these forces interact in the most important areas of union activity. In the brief space remaining, it is possible only to distill these illustrations into a more succinct, more general statement.

Starting first with the rank and file, a mass of data suggests that the members are primarily interested in their union as an agent for negotiating with the employer and administering the collective-bargaining agreement. Where these functions are involved, the members exert influences through many different channels to impose certain restraints upon their leaders. Sometimes the demands of the members are very high, even impossibly so; sometimes they can be modified by the leaders through education and persuasion. Once formed, however, these demands can be ignored only at the risk of decertification, election defeat, refusals to ratify contracts, wildcat strikes, or other forms of withholding cooperation.

The members expect little and ordinarily demand even less in other areas of union activity, such as organizing, political action, or community service. Their main interest is simply that these programs not require too large an expenditure of dues, or demand too much time and attention from union officials. To enforce this interest, members exert pressure either by refusing dues increases and special levies to pay for the programs, or by withholding their cooperation or participation, which is often essential if the programs are to succeed.

Throughout the entire range of union programs, the members tend to impose closer restraints upon local leaders than upon national officials, especially if the local organizations are small. At the national level, it is much more difficult to marshal an effective protest or to oust the incumbent officials, since opposition must be mounted in many widely scattered groups of members. But in the national as well as in the local union, the influence of the member expresses itself more insistently and through many more channels than most observers have been prepared to concede. On the whole, moreover, the influence has been much less salutary than critics of unions like to acknowledge. A candid appraisal compels the conclusion that the rank and file has contributed to most of the widely condemned union shortcomings: racial discrimination, excessive wage demands, featherbedding, and—in many instances—irresponsible strikes.

The union leader is also limited by his subordinates. In many cases, of course, the subordinate is simply a vehicle for pressures arising from the membership. Thus, local officials will resist advice or commands which, if carried out, would threaten defeat at the next local election. But subordinates can limit their superiors in ways quite independent of any rank-and-file sentiments. Local leaders may develop personal ambitions that can be furthered by resisting the international. Staff personnel may have views and priorities that conflict with those of the union leaders they serve. Local officials or staff can simply lack the ability to carry out orders effectively. In theory, of course, the higher official may have formal authority to order his subordinates about. In practice, however, the situation is not so simple. The leader must normally obtain genuine cooperation and even enthusiasm from his subordinates, and this cannot often be achieved if the leader does not accommodate himself, to some extent at least, to the abilities and desires of those whom he commands.

The environment presses in upon the union from many directions: through the policies of employers; the market pressures affecting the firm, the industry, and the entire economy; the attitudes of the public; the provisions of the law. With all its endless variety, the environment affects the union in three essential ways.

To begin with, the environment acts upon the members and shapes their outlook, their expectations, and their preferences. For example, the openness of the society and the lack of class divisions have had much to do with the unwillingness of union members to support a labor party. The educational system and the gradual evolution of community values have produced large changes in the attitudes of union members toward the Negro. The restless disaffection of the young pervades the unions as it does so many other institutions. Advertising and the widespread emphasis on material success inflate the demands that members make in collective negotiations. As a general rule, influences of this sort play their most vital role in helping to determine union goals.

The environment also affects the methods unions can use to achieve their goals and the degree of success that they will achieve. Thus, the creation of vast conglomerate firms has impelled many different unions to join in "coalition bargaining" to increase their bargaining power. In turn, the effectiveness of this strategy will be conditioned by the financial health and competitive position of the firm and its separate units, as well as by conditions in the economy as a whole. In similar fashion, labor's success in organizing mass-production industries in the thirties (after repeated failures in the past) was greatly helped by such factors as the impact of the Depression, the personnel policies of the firms involved, and the newly enacted federal law to protect union organization. Conversely, the inability of many of the same labor officials to organize the South ten years later was due to another set of social and community pressures that hampered the organizer and dulled the incentive of employees to join a union.

The environment affects the union movement in still another way by helping to shape the quality of labor leadership. The political traditions and the laws of this country insure that union leaders will be chosen by the members. This policy in turn implies that the leaders will be chosen from the ranks and will be generally representative of the membership. At the same time, the educational system, the programs of scholarships and student aid, the emphasis on social mobility, and the willingness to recognize talent whenever it appears, all create opportunities through which promising individuals can escape the shop floor and the assembly line from which tomorrow's labor leaders must be drawn. The low prestige that society accords to union leaders also helps to insure that many employees will take advantage of these opportunities instead of seeking a union post. In this way, environmental forces diminish the pool of talent available for union office.

What freedom of action remains to the union leader caught between the pressures of the environment and the demands of the rank and file? To begin with, he can experiment and innovate, at least on a modest scale. He may not always be able to launch new programs costing large sums nor will he be quick to experiment at the risk of failing to meet the critical demands imposed by his members. Moreover, his innovations will eventually have to win acceptance by the rank and file in order to survive and flourish. Nevertheless, the activities and achievements of the union will ultimately reflect the capacity of its officials to offer up new goals, new programs, and new benefits for the members to consider.

Union leaders can also do something to alter the opinions of the members and affect their attitudes toward the goals and policies of the organization. On specific trade-union issues—to accept or reject the contract; to strike or not to strike—the leader may have great influence, especially if he is popular and without vocal opposition. On more general matters of value, social attitude, and political choice, his opportunities for exerting influence may be sufficient to deserve attention, but they are not large. Where these issues are concerned, it is normally too difficult to reach the members, too hard to engage their attention seriously, too arduous to overcome all the competing messages reaching them through other media and other sources.

Finally, and perhaps most important, the leader can have the imagination to conceive of new strategies and new opoprtunities in the environment to help the union make fresh progress toward its goals. This capacity is partly a matter of knowing the environment well, but it is ultimately dependent on the intuition, the judgment, and the imagination of the leader. It is this type of influence and power that John L. Lewis demonstrated so tellingly in perceiving that the time was ripe for massive organizing in the thirties.

It is very hard to guess how much an able, imaginative leader could accomplish to make progress toward union goals. Nevertheless, it is safe to say that the process of selecting union officials—

while admirably suited for certain purposes—is not likely to produce an unusual number of leaders with exceptional vision or imagination. Indeed, one would frankly expect less talent of this sort in unions than in most other major institutions. In addition, many of the forces that press upon the labor leader are strong indeed and leave him with much less freedom of action than many critics seem to recognize. For example, those who exhort the unions to exercise wage restraint, eliminate featherbedding, or refrain from strikes seem greatly to underestimate the pressures from the members. Although most union leaders have a degree of influence over the policies of their organizations, few would stay in office very long if they slighted their members' concern for safeguards against the loss of work or ignored their desire to seek pay raises—and go on strike if need be—to keep pace with wage and price increases they see occurring all around them.

One can readily sympathize with the visions of other critics who deplore the failure of union leaders to seize opportunities to turn their talents to new fields: organizing the poor, mobilizing the members to fight for consumer protection, and taking the lead in searching for a more meaningful life for workers caught between their television set and the tedium of a semiskilled, repetitive job. In one sense, unions seem naturally suited to such tasks in view of their experience in organizing mass movements, their large memberships, and their commitment to high social purposes. Yet, critics invariably overlook the enormous difficulties involved: the members' lack of interest in undertaking ventures outside the traditional union domain, their unwillingness to see their dues expended for such purposes, the shortages of talented leadership in labor's ranks, and the pressures on existing leaders, whose time and energy are already stretched thin attending to conventional union tasks. In the face of such limitations, even a leader as gifted and energetic as Walter Reuther has been unable to make noteworthy progress in organizing the poor, expanding union membership, altering Detroit politics, or expanding the skilled job opportunities for Negro members. By underestimating these problems, liberal critics have succeeded—after two decades of biting prose—in accomplishing virtually nothing except to antagonize the union leadership.

This sketch of union behavior has clear implications for the critic's role in assessing social institutions. In reality, union members, leaders, subordinates, and environmental forces interact in such an intimate way that it is treacherous to single out one set of actors in the drama and heap responsibility upon them. Union behavior must be seen as the product of a complex, interrelated process. In order to be effective and fair, the critic must seek to identify the various centers of initiative throughout this process and suggest the actions that can be taken by each of these groups to make it easier for unions to progress toward desirable goals.

The United States Labor Force

WILLIAM S. PEIRCE AND RONALD L. OAXACA

This discussion was written especially for this volume by William Peirce and Ronald Oaxaca, who teach at Case Western Reserve University and the University of Massachusetts at Amherst, respectively.

COUNT THE NUMBER of persons "employed" in the United States in a given week; count the number of persons who were "unemployed" in the same week; add the two numbers together and you obtain the size of the "labor force".[1] According to the Current Population Survey conducted by the Bureau of the Census, in April 1970 there were 86.6 million Americans in the labor force— about 82.9 million employed (including those in the armed forces) and 3.7 million unemployed. The rest of the population (the not-in-the-labor-force group) is a potpourri of children, students not holding part-time jobs, homemakers, retired persons, person in institutions, and surviving members of the class once known as "the idle rich."

The labor force is by no means a static group. During the course of a year there are many new entrants: Some have just finished school (graduated or "dropped out"); some have seen their last child start school and have decided to look for part-time or full-time work; others may have been forced to enter or reenter the labor force because of pressing family financial needs. At the same time others have been leaving the labor force through retirement, illness, death, pregnancy, or discouragement because of inability to find a job. Thus, nearly 94 million people (16 years and over) worked or looked for work at some time

1. To be counted as "employed," a person has to work at least one hour for pay or profit or fifteen hours without pay in a family farm or business; thus homemakers are not counted as employed. Also, those temporarily absent from their jobs due to illness, vacation, bad weather, labor-management disputes, or personal reasons are counted as employed. To be counted as "unemployed," a person must not be "employed," must have looked for work in the previous four weeks, and in addition must look for work during the given week. For further details see any issue of *Employment and Earnings*, U.S. Department of Labor.

during 1969, yet the labor force never exceeded 88 million people at any time during that year.

The size of the labor force depends both on the size of the population and on the proportion of the population who want to work. In view of the marked increase in the total population, it is certainly not surprising that the labor force in 1970 was larger than in 1900; what is rather remarkable is that the proportion of the population of working age (14 years and older) in the labor force has changed relatively little over a seventy-year period. Between 1900 and 1970 the working-age population increased from 51.2 million to 147.6 million, and the labor force increased from 28.1 million to 86.6 million. Dividing the labor force by the population gives us the labor-force participation rate—54.9 percent in 1900 and 58.7 percent in 1970. Furthermore, the participation rate has averaged 55 percent over a seventy-year period when examined at ten-year intervals. This constancy has led L. R. Klein and R. F. Kosobud to refer to the participation rate as one of the "great ratios of economics."

The long-run constancy of the participation rate certainly does not mean that the size of the labor force is rigidly fixed at any moment; in the short run, the size of the labor force depends on many things, including the demand for labor. As World War II showed, many additional persons, including the retired and handicapped, can be drawn into the labor force if social pressures and the demand for their services are sufficiently strong. There is also a body of evidence indicating that periods of unemployment can retard the growth of the labor force by discouraging some people from continuing to seek work.

AGE-SEX COMPOSITION OF THE LABOR FORCE

Nor does the constancy of the overall participation rate imply that the composition of the labor force has remained constant. The relative contribution that any age-sex group of the population makes to the labor force depends both on the proportion of the whole population in that group and on the group's labor-force participation rate. Table 1 shows the age-sex composition of the labor force in various census years; Chart 1 shows the participation rates of selected groups. From the chart and table, several interesting conclusions can be drawn:

1. The simple notion that the labor force is made up of adult

TABLE 1. *The Age-Sex Composition of the United States Labor Force* (*percent*)

Age-Sex Group	1970	1960	1950	1940	1930	1920	1910	1900
Males 14–19	5	4	4	5	6	7	9	10
Males 20–24	8	7	8	9	10	10	12	12
Males 25–64	47	54	57	58	58	59	57	56
Males 65+	3	3	4	3	4	4	3	4
All Males	63	68	73	76	78	80	80	82
Women 14–19	4	3	2	2	3	4	4	5
Women 20–24	6	4	4	5	5	4	4	4
Women 25–64	26	24	20	16	13	12	10	9
Women 65+	1	1	1	1	1	—	1	—
All Women	37	32	27	24	22	20	20	18
(All married women 16+)	(21)	(18)	(13)	(7)	(6)	(5)	(5)	(3)

SOURCES: Clarence D. Long, *The Labor Force Under Changing Income and Employment* (Princeton University Press for the National Bureau of Economic Research, 1958), Tables A-2 and A-6. *U.S. Census of Population 1960*, "U.S. Summary, Detailed Characteristics," Table 194. *Employment and Earnings*, vol. 16, no. 11, May 1970, Tables A-3, A-27. *Manpower Report of the President*, April 1971, Table B-4.

males is only about half right. Males aged 25–64 have averaged about 55.8 percent of the labor force.

2. Younger males play a considerably less important role in the labor force now than they did in 1900. The chart indicates the rapid decline in participation rates between 1900 and 1940 of male teenagers. This is largely attributable to the increasing proportion of this age group enrolled in school and the corresponding decrease in full-time job-holding. In recent years the participation rate has increased slightly as part-time work has become more common for students. The decrease in participation of males aged 20–24 (not shown on the chart) came somewhat later than that of the teenagers and has not been as rapid. The effect of these decreases in participation rates can be seen in Table 1, which indicates that males aged 14–24 contributed only 13 percent of the labor force in 1970, compared with 22 percent in 1900.

3. At the other end of the age span, the participation of males 65 years old and over in the labor force has also shown a long-run (but not unbroken) decrease. The very large decrease in participation rates between 1930 and 1940 may reflect a tendency for older men who could not find jobs during the depression to retire rather than continue what many no doubt regarded as a vain

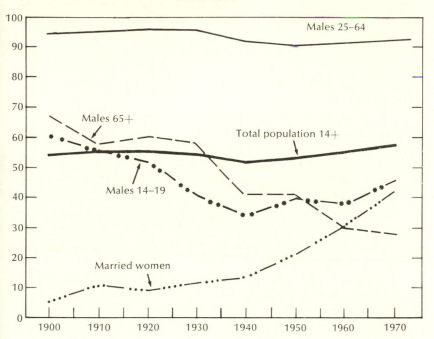

quest for work. The manpower demands of World War II undoubtedly kept many men in the labor force beyond their normal retirement but after 1950 the participation rate resumed its downward trend. Even though the participation rate for older males has decreased, this group's proportion of the total labor force has not declined. The explanation, of course, is that the number of men aged 65 and older has been growing so rapidly that, even though a smaller percentage of them are working, they continue to constitute nearly as large a proportion of the total labor force as formerly.

4. The most striking and significant changes have occurred in the labor-force participation of married women (the term "married women" here refers to "married women with husbands present"). The urgent need for additional labor in World War II undoubtedly played some role in breaking down the prejudice against married women working outside the home. However, as the chart indicates, the participation rate for married women had already increased from 5.6 percent in 1900 to 13.8 percent by 1940. By 1970 the rate was 40.8 percent.

In addition to attitudes, the factors associated with the increased participation of women relate to time, opportunity, and technology. One time-saver has been the decrease in average family size. A common pattern today is for the woman to continue work after marriage until the first child is born; retire from the labor force until the youngest child is in school; and then re-enter the labor force to supplement family income. A decrease in the number of children can shorten the interval during which the woman stays out of the labor force or lighten housekeeping burdens enough to permit part-time work outside the home.

Another factor has been the decrease in the percentage of the population living in rural areas. For example, in 1960 the participation rate for married women living on farms was 21.9 percent, compared with 32.3 percent for married women living in urban areas. This certainly does not imply that the typical married woman living on a farm does less work than her urban counterpart, but only that her work is less likely to be counted as participation in the labor force. From the standpoint of obtaining paid employment the urban woman has two advantages: She is free of many of the chores of a farm household, and she is also more likely to be living in an area where there are offices, shops, and factories, where the opportunity to find a job is greater.

Changing technology has been still more important. Within the home, new products (for example, prepared foods and inexpensive ready-to-wear clothing) have saved vast amounts of time for American women. Tasks formerly carried out in the home are now done in factories, and homemakers to an increasing extent have joined the measured labor force. The increase in the number of jobs which are light, clean, and relatively pleasant has no doubt induced many women to enter the labor force rather than remain at home.

THE OCCUPATIONAL COMPOSITION OF THE LABOR FORCE

The same kinds of technical change that have played such a major part in increasing the participation rate of married women have also led to important changes in the occupational composition of the entire labor force.

The "typical worker" in 1900 was either a farmworker or an industrial blue-collar worker. The number of workers in each

TABLE 2. *The Labor Force, by Major Occupation Group, 1900–1970*
(*percent*)

Major Occupation Group	1970	1960	1950	1940	1930	1920	1910	1900
White-collar workers	47.8	42.3	36.6	31.1	29.4	24.9	21.3	17.6
Professional, technical, and kindred workers	14.1	11.4	8.6	7.5	6.8	5.4	4.7	4.3
Managers, officials, and proprietors, except farm	10.2	8.4	8.7	7.3	7.4	6.6	6.6	5.8
Clerical and kindred workers	17.5	15.0	12.3	9.6	8.9	8.0	5.3	3.0
Sales workers	6.0	7.5	7.0	6.7	6.3	4.9	4.7	4.5
Blue-collar workers	35.7	39.6	41.1	39.8	39.6	40.2	38.2	35.8
Craftsmen, foremen, and kindred workers	12.8	14.3	14.1	12.0	12.8	13.0	11.6	10.5
Operatives and kindred workers	18.1	19.9	20.4	18.4	15.8	15.6	14.6	12.8
Laborers, except mine and farm	4.8	5.4	6.6	9.4	11.0	11.6	12.0	12.5
Service workers	12.5	11.8	10.5	11.7	9.8	7.8	9.6	9.0
Private household workers	2.0	2.8	2.6	4.7	4.1	3.3	5.0	5.4
Service workers, except private household	10.5	9.0	7.9	7.1	5.7	4.5	4.6	3.6
Farm workers	4.0	6.3	11.8	17.4	21.2	27.0	30.9	37.5
Farmers and farm managers	—	3.9	7.4	10.4	12.4	15.3	16.5	19.9
Farm laborers and foremen	—	2.4	4.4	7.0	8.8	11.7	14.4	17.7

SOURCES: Manpower Report of the President 1963, Table G-5; *Employment and Earnings*, Vol. 16, No. 11, May 1970, Tables A-10 and A-18.

group was about equal and, as Table 2 shows, about three-quarters of the labor force found employment in one of these two occupational categories. Since then the relative importance of jobs requiring heavy manual labor has decreased markedly. Farmworkers, who comprised 37.5 percent of the labor force in 1900, declined in relative importance to about 4 percent of the labor force in 1970. In fact, the absolute number of farmworkers has decreased in each census since 1910. Unskilled laborers comprised 12.5 percent of the labor force in 1900 and nearly as large a proportion in 1930, but since then they have decreased to about 5 percent of the labor force. Blue-collar workers as a whole have just about maintained their share (35–40 percent) of the labor force. This has been due to an increase in the number of (semiskilled) operatives and (skilled) craftsmen sufficient to compensate for the decreasing importance of unskilled labor.

The white-collar occupations have shown by far the greatest growth. This category grew steadily from 17.6 percent of the labor force in 1900 to 47.8 percent in 1970. The jobs in this category vary greatly in pay, educational requirements, and prestige. Included here are not only doctors, lawyers, scientists, teachers, and managers, but also office workers and low-paid technicians—not to mention professional athletes. More than half of all employed women are in this broad occupational category.

The other major occupational category, service workers, consists of two groups showing different trends. Private household workers ("domestics") have decreased greatly in relative importance since 1900. During the same period, the proportion of the population engaged in nonhousehold services has nearly tripled. The combined effect of these trends has been an increase in the proportion of service workers, from 9 to 12.5 percent of the population.

No single stereotype characterizes the "typical worker" of 1970. He might be a skilled or semiskilled blue-collar worker, but he is more likely to wear a white collar and work in an office. And the "he" may very well be a "she."

Changes in the occupational composition of the labor force can be traced to two sources. In the first place, the relative number of people employed in various industries changes. In part this results from the uneven pace of labor-saving innovation in various industries. For example, total employment in the motor-vehicles and parts industries decreased about 20 percent between 1955 and 1963, although the number of vehicles produced was nearly the same. In contrast, education shows no sign of using less labor per student. In part, also, the change in the industrial distribution of employment can be traced to changing allocations of the consumer dollar.

Secondly, the occupational structure changes simply because of changes in the "occupational mixes" of given industries. An excavating contractor in 1900, for example, employed mostly unskilled labor. In 1970 he employed skilled operators of heavy equipment and semiskilled truck drivers. In some of the "automated" industries we have been hearing so much about, semiskilled machine tenders and even white-collar workers have been displaced.

For those who want to look ahead, the Bureau of Labor Statistics has prepared projections [2] that, in the main, assume a continuation of the trends noted above. Unfortunately for the makers and users of such projections, however, unforeseen breaks in labor-market trends have a habit of occurring.

2. See *Manpower Report of the President,* April 1971, Appendix E.

Part two   Efficiency Issues

Labor Unions and Economic Policy

MILTON FRIEDMAN

Milton Friedman is professor of economics at the University of Chicago. This widely discussed essay was originally published in 1951 in a volume entitled The Impact of the Union.

LABOR UNIONS are important political and economic institutions that significantly affect both public and private actions. This fact raises serious and difficult problems for economic policy. At the same time, laymen and economists alike tend, in my view, to exaggerate greatly the extent to which labor unions affect the structure and level of wage rates. This fact is one of the most serious obstacles to a balanced judgment about appropriate public policies toward unions. . . .

This paper is concerned almost entirely with the long-run effect of unions on the structure and level of wage rates and thereby on the allocation of resources. From this strictly economic point of view, labor unions and enterprise monopolies are conceptually similar if not identical phenomena and have similar effects. In particular, the economic significance of both tends to be exaggerated for much the same reasons, and the fact of exaggeration tends to have much the same implications for policy. In my view, appropriate public policy calls for like treatment of both forms of monopoly—treatment designed to keep their extent and importance to a minimum. . . .

SOME IMPLICATIONS OF ORTHODOX ECONOMIC THEORY

The power of unions, as of any other monopoly, is ultimately limited by the elasticity of the demand curve for the monopolized services. Unions have significant potential power only if this demand curve is fairly inelastic at what would otherwise be the competitive price. Even then, of course, they must also be able to control either the supply of workers or the wage rate employers will offer workers.

Demand for Labor · The theory of joint demand developed by Marshall is in some ways the most useful tool of orthodox economic theory for understanding the circumstances under which the demand curve will be inelastic. It will be recalled that Marshall emphasized that the demand for one of a number of jointly demanded items is the more inelastic, (1) the more essential the given item is in the production of the final product, (2) the more inelastic the demand for the final product, (3) the smaller the fraction of total cost accounted for by the item in question, and (4) the more inelastic the supply of co-operating factors.[1] The most significant of these items for the analysis of unions are the essentiality of the factor and the percentage of total costs accounted for by the factor. Now, a factor is likely to be far more essential in the short run than in the long run. Let a union be organized and let it suddenly raise the wage rate. Employment of the type of labor in question is likely to shrink far less at first than it will over the longer run, when it is possible to make fuller adjustment to the change in wage rate. This adjustment will take the form of substitution of other factors for this one, both directly in the production of each product, and indirectly in consumption as the increased price of the products of unionized labor leads consumers to resort to alternative means of satisfying their wants. This simple point is, at one and the same time, important in understanding how unions can have substantial power and how their power is sharply limited in the course of time.

The importance of the percentage of total cost accounted for by the factor leads one to predict that a union may be expected to be strongest and most potent when it is composed of a class of workers whose wages make up only a small part of the total cost of the product they produce—a condition satisfied, along with essentiality, by highly skilled workers. This is the reason

1. Alfred Marshall, *Principles of Economics* (8th ed.; Macmillan, 1920), pp. 385-386.

why economic theorists have always been inclined to predict that craft unions would tend to be the most potent. This implication of the joint-demand analysis seems to have been confirmed by experience. While industrial unions have by no means been impotent, craft unions have in general been in a stronger economic position and have maintained it for longer periods. . . .

Supply of Labor and Control over Wage Rates · Another line along which orthodox economic analysis has some interesting implications is the role of so-called restrictive practices. It is clear that if a union can reduce the supply of persons available for jobs, it will thereby tend to raise the wage rate. Indeed, this will be the only way of raising the wage rate if the union cannot exercise any direct control over the wage rate itself. For example, in a field like medicine, there is no significant way of exercising direct control over fees charged, or over annual incomes of physicians. The only effective control is over the number of physicians. In consequence, medicine is a clear example of the kind of situation that is usually envisaged in which the wage rate or its equivalent is raised by deliberate control over entry into the occupation.

This line of reasoning has led to the view that, in general, unions may be regarded as exercising control over the wage rate primarily by controlling the supply of workers and that, in consequence, the so-called restrictive practices—high union initiation fees, discriminatory provisions for entrance into unions, seniority rules, etc.—have the economic function of reducing the supply of entrants so as to raise wage rates. This is an erroneous conception of the function of these restrictive practices. They clearly cannot serve this function without a closed or preferential shop, which already implies control over employers derived from sources other than control over entrance into unions. To see the function of these practices and the associated closed shop, let us suppose that the wage rate can be fixed above its competitive level by direct means, for example, by legal enactment of a minimum wage rate. This will necessarily mean that fewer jobs will be available than otherwise and fewer jobs than persons seeking jobs. This excess supply of labor must be disposed of somehow—the jobs must be rationed among the seekers for jobs. And this is the important economic function the so-called restrictive practices play. They are a means of rationing the limited number of jobs among eager applicants. Since the opportunity to work at a wage rate above the competitive level has considerable economic value, it is understandable that the restrictive practices are important and the source of much dispute.

The question remains how the wage rate can be controlled directly by means other than legal enactment of a minimum wage rate. To do this, unions must be able to exercise control over employers—they must be able to prevent existing employers from undercutting the union wage rate, as well as the entry of new employers who would do so. They must somehow be able to force all employers to offer the union wage rate and no less. The devices whereby this is done are numerous and can hardly be fully enumerated here. However, one feature of the various devices whereby wage rates are directly enforced or entry into an occupation limited is essential for our purposes, namely, the extent to which they depend on political assistance. Perhaps the extreme example is again medicine, in which practice of the profession is restricted to those licensed by the state and licensure in turn is in general placed in the hands of the profession itself. State licensure applies in similar fashion to dentists, lawyers, plumbers, beauticians, barbers, morticians, and a host of other occupations too numerous to list. Wherever there is licensure, it is almost invariably in the hands of the existing members of the occupation, who almost as invariably seek to use it to limit entry. Of course, in many cases, these techniques are largely ineffective, either because it is not feasible to restrict drastically the number of licenses granted, or because it is possible to evade the licensure provisions. But they do exemplify how political power can be used to control entry directly. Only slightly removed from this kind of licensure provision and in many ways far more effective is local political support through building codes, health regulations, health ordinances, and the like, all of which serve numerous craft unions as a means of preventing nonunion workers from engaging in their fields through substitution or elimination of materials or techniques, and of preventing potential employers from undercutting the union wage rate. It is no accident that strong unions are found in railways, along with federal regulation. Again, union actions involving actual or potential physical violence or coercion, such as mass picketing and the like, could hardly take place were it not for the unspoken acquiescence of the authorities. Thus, whether directly in the form of specific laws giving power to union groups or indirectly in the form of the atmosphere and attitude of law enforcement, direct control over union wage rates is closely connected to the degree of political assistance unions can command.

Here again, there is a very close parallel between labor unions on the one hand and industrial monopolies on the other. In both cases, widespread monopolies are likely to be temporary and susceptible of dissolution unless they can call to their aid the political power of the state.

THE SIGNIFICANCE OF UNION-MADE ALTERATIONS IN THE STRUCTURE OF WAGE RATES

It would take a major research project—and, incidentally, one that is very much needed—to get a reasonably precise quantitative estimate of the extent to which unions have changed the structure of wage rates. Fortunately, no such precise estimate is required for our purposes. All that is needed is some indication of the order of magnitude of the effect, and this can be obtained fairly readily.

Total union membership is currently about 16 million, or something over one-quarter of the labor force. On the basis of our preceding analysis, however, it seems likely that many if not most members are in unions that have had only a negligible effect on wage rates. In the long view, it seems likely that unions have made wage rates significantly different from what they otherwise would have been, primarily in construction, railroads, printing trades, and in general the areas in which old-line craft unions are strong. Total membership in craft unions is probably not over 6 million, and by no means all these can be supposed to be in unions that have affected wage rates significantly. To this needs to be added persons in organizations like the American Medical Association that are the economic equivalents of unions though not counted formally as such, and members of those industrial unions that have had a significant effect on wage rates. Thus probably not over 10 percent and certainly not over 20 percent of the labor force can be supposed to have had their wages significantly affected by the existence of unions.[2]

2. It is often asserted that nonunion members have had their wages raised because of the "pattern" set by the unions. This may have some validity for workers highly competitive with union workers, but in the main, the

It is very much more difficult to say how much unions have affected wage rates. If the experience in medicine can be taken as representative, even quite strong unions have not in the long run raised relative wage rates by more than about 15 or 20 percent above the levels that would have prevailed without unions; and this would certainly seem like a high estimate of the average effect.

Roughly, then, we might assess the order of magnitude of unions' effect on the structure of wages by saying that perhaps 10 percent of the labor force has had its wages raised by some 15 percent, implying that the remainder of the labor force has had its wage rates reduced by some 1 to 4 percent, the exact amount depending on the relative wages of the two groups. Now this is by no means an unimportant effect; the danger of underrating it should be avoided as much as the danger of exaggerating it. Yet I suspect it will strike most readers as small, relative to their implicit expectations. Perhaps most readers, unpersuaded by what precedes, will regard it as a gross understatement, reflecting simply my own biases and inability to read plain fact. This may be correct, but I urge the reader to withhold final judgment until he has read the section that follows, which seeks to explain why supposedly plain fact may be exceedingly misleading. . . .

WHY THE EFFECT OF UNIONS ON THE STRUCTURE OF WAGES TENDS TO BE EXAGGERATED

If one accepts the crude kind of evidence presented in the preceding section,[3] one is inclined to ask why casual observation

---

assertions are supported by neither economic analysis nor empirical evidence. The observed general similarity of many wage movements in union and nonunion areas is better interpreted as the result of common influences from the side of demand. The presence of unions in some areas merely means that wage changes that would have taken place anyway are made through the medium of the unions. In general, one would expect that any rise in the wage rates of certain classes of workers secured by unions would tend to lower wage rates of other workers because of the increased competition of workers for jobs. But this should not be added to the effects considered in the text, which is concerned with changes in relative wage rates; it is simply the other side of the coin.

3. [The section to which Professor Friedman refers was omitted by the editor because of space limitation. It contained comparisons of rates of change of money wages and prices during three war periods: the Civil War, World War I, and World War II. While stressing imperfections in

leads most observers—even trained ones—to exaggerate the extent to which unions affect the structure of wages. Alternatively, one may seek to determine whether the effect of unions is exaggerated by asking whether there are any reasons why observers should, on balance, exaggerate them. The comments that follow will serve either purpose.

In a dynamic world, economic forces are always arising that tend to change relative wage rates. Shifts in demand for final products, changes in techniques, discovery of new resources, and so on, all produce changes in the demand for and supply of labor of various grades, and hence changes in wage rates. In the absence of unions, these forces will operate more or less directly on wage rates. Given unions, the same forces will be present but they will operate indirectly on wage rates through the mediation of the union. For example, a change in demand that would have led to an increased wage rate in the absence of the union is likely to do so in the presence of the union only through the intervention of the union. Strikes may be required to produce wage rises that would have occurred in the absence of the union. This change in the process whereby the underlying forces work themselves out leads to unions being regarded as causes of changes rather than as intermediaries. In many cases, so to speak, unions are simply thermometers registering the heat rather than furnaces producing the heat. This is particularly obvious during periods of inflationary pressure. It clearly must be significant at other times as well, and a number of examples illustrating this point have already been given.

A second closely related reason for the exaggeration of the significance of unions is that, like monopolies in general, unions are newsworthy. The fact that economic forces work through unions means that these forces work through a limited number of identifiable persons and thereby become capable of generating "personal" news. Moreover, since union-management dealings can only take place at discrete intervals of time and with respect to matters of some moment, forces that would work themselves out slowly, gradually, and unnoticeably accumulate until they come to a head. They must then be dealt with at one point in

the data and the absence of controls for other factors, Friedman interprets the relatively modest differences in the rates of wage increase as consistent with his assessment of the order of magnitude of union impact. *Editor.*]

time and at a stage when the consequences are dramatic and obvious. On the other hand, the forces that bring about wage changes in nonunionized areas operate subtly, impersonally, and continuously, and so tend to go unnoticed.

In the third place, whereas union actions are newsworthy and call attention to themselves, the indirect effects of union actions are not. These indirect effects to some extent reflect the harm unions do in altering the allocation of resources, and to this extent lead to underestimation of the significance of unions. But more important, I believe, are the indirect effects whereby the apparent influence and importance of unions are undermined and the forces which unions bottle up find expression—whereby, that is, the demand for the services of union members is rendered highly elastic. These indirect effects work through devious and subterranean channels and attract little notice. They consist of the somewhat more rapid expansion of an industry here and an industry there, gradual changes in the kinds of workers hired, gradual changes in the consumption patterns of millions of people, the devotion of increased attention to one kind of research rather than another, and so on and on in endless detail. The strike of union typographers in Chicago, for example, attracted great attention, as did the effects of the union in preceding years on typographical wages. The slow but steady development of substitute processes of reproduction, which was undoubtedly stimulated in considerable measure by the existence of the union, attracted little or no attention. Yet this is one of the more dramatic and obvious indirect effects. Moreover, these indirect effects tend to work themselves out slowly, in the long run, and so are difficult to connect with the forces responsible for them.

These brief remarks about the factors tending to exaggerated estimates of the role of unions apply equally to industrial monopolies and serve to explain why the role of industrial monopolies tends likewise to be exaggerated. One striking illustration of both tendencies is that individuals asked to list the most important industries in the United States will practically never list domestic service. Yet the income produced through the hiring of domestic servants is year in and year out considerably larger than that produced in either the automobile industry or coal mining, and the number of employees is much greater than in the two industries combined.[4] The explanation is obvious in light of the comments above. The automobile industry calls attention to itself by the size and importance of its separate firms, by the amount of advertising it engages in, and, in the last few years, by the disputes that arise between the firms and their organized employees. The millions of domestic servants working for their separate individual employers call little or no public attention to themselves.

The bias introduced into our judgment of the effects of unions by this difference in the capacity of unionized and nonunionized sectors to attract attention is dramatized by a war and postwar increase in the compensation of domestic servants of roughly the same order of magnitude as the increase in the compensation of coal miners and much greater than the increase in the compensation of auto workers. Average annual earnings per full-time employee were 2.72 times as large in 1948 as in 1939 for domestic servants; 2.83 for soft-coal workers; and 1.98 for auto workers.[5] Yet, aside from individual grumbling, the rise in the price of domestic service has attracted little attention and has certainly not been attributed to the influence of unions. The comparable or smaller rises in the wage rates of coal miners and auto workers have attracted far more attention and have commonly been attributed almost entirely to union activity.

The abnormally large rise in the wages of domestic servants and coal miners, like the even larger rise in the wages of farm laborers,[6] is, in my view, attributable to essentially the same factors. All three occupations are relatively unattractive; in-

4. See National Income Supplement, *Survey of Current Business*, July, 1947, Tables 13, 24, and 25.

5. National Income Supplement, *Survey of Current Business*, July, 1947, Table 26; and *ibid.*, July, 1949, p. 21. The figures used for domestic servants are for the industry designated, "Services, Private households"; for soft-coal workers, for the industry designated, "Mining, Bituminous and other soft coal"; for auto workers, for the industry designated, "Manufacturing, Automobile and automobile equipment." The ratios for coal miners are not comparable with those in Table 1, because based on average annual earnings, instead of hourly earnings, of a somewhat different group of workers, and because the basic figures come from different sources. The change in the figures used as the basis of the ratios is required in order to have figures comparable to those for domestic servants.

6. The ratio for farm labor comparable to those just cited for the other groups is 3.45. This is based on the sources listed in the preceding footnote for the industry designated, "Agriculture, forestry, and fisheries, Farms."

dividuals leave them gladly when alternative employment opportunities are available—and such opportunities were relatively plentiful during the period in question, so that migration from the respective industries was extremely easy. Substantial increases in wages were therefore required in all three industries to hold even as many workers as were in fact kept attached to them. It therefore seems very likely that the increase in the wages of coal miners would have been of much the same order of magnitude in the absence of the union, which implies that this is also true of the increase in the price of coal. Further support for this view is provided by the World War I experience, when nonunionized coal miners experienced a larger percentage increase in wage rates than unionized coal miners.[7] Yet given the existence of a strong union, the World War II wage increases had to take place through the medium of the union and could be obtained only through strikes, and so the general impression arose that the coal miners' union has been extremely effective in raising wage rates and has succeeded in pushing wage rates well above the level that would otherwise have prevailed.

I do not wish to argue that the United Mine Workers' Union had no effect on the war and postwar rise in wages. I do say that its effect was of the second order of importance; perhaps it was responsible for something like 10 to 30 percentage points of the 183-percent increase in annual earnings from 1939 to 1948. Its more significant effect will probably be in delaying or preventing a decline that underlying economic conditions may tend to bring about, and this may already be in process. . . .

CONCLUSIONS FOR POLICY

The tendency to exaggerate the effect of unions on the structure of wage rates, and similarly of industrial monopolies on the structure of product prices, has a number of possible implications for policy that to some extent are contradictory. The exaggerated importance attached to unions may make it appear that they are dominant long before they really are; or

7. Some of these statements are based on as yet unpublished results of research by Albert Rees to be incorporated in his dissertation, *The Effect of Collective Bargaining on Wage and Price Levels in the Basic Steel and Bituminous Coal Industries, 1945–48.*

that their ultimate dominance is so inevitable that it is hopeless to seek to curb their further development. Evidence that such attitudes can readily develop is provided by the widespread, though in my view mistaken, feeling that industrial monopoly is already so important, and further extension of monopoly so inevitable, that it is hopeless to seek to reverse the alleged trend. This view about industrial monopoly not only is evidence that exaggeration of the economic importance of unions may lead to a similar view about unions, it also directly supports the development of a feeling that the further growth of unions is inevitable since unions are widely believed—whether rightly or wrongly is irrelevant for the present issue—a consequence of, or a desirable offset to, industrial monopoly.

A second possible effect, and in my view a far more salutary one, is that the exaggeration of the importance of labor unions will give rise to movements to limit their power and importance long before they have been able to achieve enough importance to exercise any significant or irreversible influence on the allocation of resources.

A third possible effect, closely linked with the first, is that overestimation of the urgency of the union problem will lead to unnecessary public policies of control and regulation that will push the economy in the direction of centralization of power. An example is the repeated proposal—made sometimes by the right, sometimes by the left—for compulsory arbitration of labor disputes.

The tendency of inflation to strengthen the political and economic importance of unions has obvious implications for policy. It adds yet another potent reason for seeking to counter the widespread inflationary bias that has been developing in our institutions and our attitudes. It increases the urgency of developing and putting into effect stabilization policies that are directed equally at the twin evils of inflation and deflation. At the same time, it calls for no action specifically directed at unions as such.

Finally, if we can curb inflation, the preceding analysis suggests rather optimistic conclusions about the possibility of developing effective policies with respect to labor unions as such. It suggests that these monopolies are likely to be weaker and less widely pervasive than one might assume offhand; that there are important economic forces working subtly and in-directly to limit their power; and that their effectiveness hinges in considerable measure on the degree of political support and assistance that they can command. It follows that it may be possible to keep in check the power of unions to affect the prices of either products or factors without any very drastic measures of a kind that are likely to be inconsistent with our general belief in personal freedom to organize. If, indeed, the current power of unions is in no small measure based upon positive acts of assistance by political authorities, the mere removal of these acts of assistance without the addition of any punitive or repressive measures might prevent any further extension of the influence of unions on the allocation of re-sources, and perhaps start a slow trend in the opposite direction. Once again the analogy with industrial monopolies is significant. In both cases, we are inclined to exaggerate the importance of monopoly, and to overstate its strength in the absence of direct political encouragement. In both cases, the establishment of a general atmosphere of belief in and respect for competitive forces and elimination of special privileges for special groups would go a long way toward preventing any undesirable eco-nomic growth of monopoly power.

It therefore seems to me highly desirable for policy purposes to emphasize the similarity and identity of enterprise and labor monopoly, and the importance of withholding direct political support from either. Thus, I would argue that it is highly important to have labor monopoly covered by the Sherman Antitrust Act, less because I have a clear conception of specific positive acts that could thereby be taken to reduce the power of unions than because such action emphasizes the identity of industrial monopolies and labor unions and the need for like treatment of them.

These optimistic conclusions about the possibility of keep-ing the power of unions in check do not imply any equally op-timistic predictions that we shall do so. The economic power of unions, though exaggerated, is nonetheless already significant and important, and so is their political power. Inflation, how-ever regrettable, seems likely, and with it a substantial further strengthening of the political and economic power of unions. For decades there has been an intellectual flight from the market toward direct state intervention in economic affairs—entirely aside from the influence of the growth of unions in this direction. There are, I believe, signs that this intellectual movement has reached its apex and has been reversed; but this may be no more than wishful thinking, or itself a temporary concomitant of postwar prosperity. In any event, it is as yet no more than a slight break in the clouds.

Labor and Antitrust

ARTHUR J. GOLDBERG

Arthur J. Goldberg was general counsel of the Industrial Union Department of the AFL–CIO when this article appeared in the IUD Digest in the winter of 1958. He has since served on the Supreme Court and as Secretary of Labor in the Kennedy Administration.

THE ULTIMATE OBJECTIVE of those who cry out against "labor monopoly" is to put our unions under the federal antitrust laws.

Should this objective ever be accomplished, organized labor will be weakened to a point of almost complete ineffectiveness. National and international unions will be prohibited from bargaining for their members at the plant level and all traces of company-wide negotiating will be eliminated. All this will be done under the guise of monopoly busting.

Employees working for any of the multi-plant employers who dominate the American economy will be restrained from using their collective strength in bettering their wages and working conditions. Instead, workers will be forced to bargain directly with the plant where they are employed as if that plant was a separate entity, completely devoid of the employer's other interests.

For the great majority of organized workers, the enactment of such legislation will mean a return to the nineteenth century when employers with vast holdings held tremendous economic power.

Those who would return to the so-called "good old days" have resurrected the charge of "labor monopoly" as a front for their real goal. If they can convince the American public that labor is a monopoly, then "protecting the public interest" will necessitate placing this "monopoly" under restrictions of anti-trust legislation.

Like the phrase "right to work," "labor monopoly" is now being drummed into the public mind as the first part of this anti-union campaign. Both phrases are equally misleading.

As "right to work" has nothing to do with a worker's right to a job, "labor monopoly" has no connection with our nation's concept of monopolistic practices.

The American public considers "monopoly" a bad word. We say that monopolies are bad—whether created by business organizations or by business organizations in conspiracy with labor organizations. Too often, however, we do not stop to analyze the reasons behind our condemnation of monopolies.

Essentially, our argument with monopoly stems from the fact that competition is economically desirable, and should be the major regulating force in a free-enterprise economy.

We oppose monopolies because we regard it as undesirable for a manufacturer to have complete control over a product, enabling him to raise prices above those prevailing in a truly competitive system. We say that such control enables the manufacturer to gain excessive profits at the expense of the public.

There are, however, areas where we recognize the fact that competition among suppliers is undesirable. For example, we do not object to one supplier of electric power, a single telephone service or a one-ownership urban transportation system. Similarly, our patent laws give inventors protection against their competitors for a limited period of time.

In such areas, we do not ordinarily apply the epithet "monopoly," although in a technical sense monopoly does exist. We do not use the term because in these areas the lack of competition is considered socially desirable.

The same type of thinking must also apply to the charge of "labor monopoly." If a labor union is to be considered an undesirable monopoly, it must be undesirable because it suppresses or destroys competition socially beneficial to our economy.

What type of competition does a labor union destroy? Competition among whom? These are questions that must be answered if the charge of "labor monopoly" is to be considered seriously.

Technically speaking, of course, any labor union is a monopoly in the limited sense that it eliminates competition between employees for the available jobs in a particular plant or industry. By concerted economic action, these workers attempt to increase the wage at which the employer will be able to purchase their labor.

If the monopoly concept is to be applied to unions—under

this false notion—all labor organizations should be forbidden and replaced by periodic auctions at which jobs can be parceled out to those qualified persons willing to supply their labor at the lowest wage.

Unions must be eliminated, under this theory, because the very purpose of labor organizations is to limit the power of an employer to drive down wage rates and enforce substandard working conditions.

If this is not the type of competition envisioned by those who speak the loudest of "labor monopolies," there would seem to be only two other types of competition they seek to encourage. These are: competition between unions to see which will supply labor at the lowest rate; and competition between employers in the sale of their products, based strictly on a difference in labor costs.

Neither of these alternatives will stand the test of careful scrutiny. No one really proposes to establish an economic system under which unions would compete with each other to supply labor at the lowest possible cost.

No responsible social critic believes that competition among manufacturers should be carried on, not on the basis of relative efficiency or ability to produce, but on the manufacturer's ability to obtain the lowest possible labor rates. The social advantage of competition is that it rewards the most efficient producer and thus guarantees the optimum use of our economic resources. There is no social advantage to be gained by allowing manufacturers to compete on the basis of sweatshop wages.

Even harder to rationalize than the question of competition is the placing of human labor in the same category as any other commodity.

There are obvious social reasons for distinguishing between the purchase and sale of commodities and the employment of workers. The owner of a commodity is not selling an object that is part of himself. He is selling property.

If the owner of a commodity is not satisfied with the price he is offered, he can generally withhold its sale until a better price is offered. But the worker is not selling a commodity. He is selling a part of himself—his own skill, strength and energy. The value of his labor, if withheld from the market, is lost and cannot be recovered.

From a practical standpoint, the individual worker cannot withdraw his labor from the market for any length of time. Without a union, he is completely at the mercy of the buyer—his employer. Since the worker must support his family and eat each day, he has no alternative but to accept whatever is offered unless he has the protection afforded by collective bargaining.

Even if the laborer had a withholding power equal to that of his employer he would generally, in the absence of labor organizations, have little knowledge of the market value of his labor.

Prior to the advent of unionism, there never was such a thing as a market value of labor. This was partially attributable to the worker's lack of knowledge of the best available opportunities and also because workers cannot ship themselves to whatever place offers them the highest wage in the way the manufacturers can transport commodities.

In the days before unions, because workers had no bargaining power there was no real competition. There was, rather, a genuine monopoly on the part of employers who could dictate the price at which labor was paid and who were not restricted by market conditions.

Until 1840, labor was considered a commodity comparable with any other product. As such, the courts held that an organization of workers to increase the price of their labor was *per se* a restraint of trade and illegal.

Beginning with the landmark decision of Chief Justice Shaw in the famous Massachusetts case of *Commonwealth* vs. *Hunt* (1842), however, the courts came to realize that the public policy against restraints of trade in commodities did not justify a ruling that the voluntary organization of workingmen was a restraint of trade and a monopoly.

This judicial recognition that the antitrust concepts do not apply in the labor market has been reinforced by repeated legislative action.

Section Six of the Clayton Act—passed in 1914—declares that "the labor of a human being is not a commodity or article of commerce" and that labor unions shall not "be held or construed to be illegal combinations or conspiracies in restraint of trade under the antitrust laws."

The Wagner Act set forth two basic reasons for distinguishing between a combination of businessmen to raise prices and a combination of workers to raise wages. The act declared that the inequality of bargaining power between employers and individual employees depresses wage rates and that low wages are detrimental to the national economy.

This section of the Wagner Act was included without change in the Taft-Hartley Act of 1947 and remains, to this day, as originally enacted.

Congress has long recognized that workers combine into unions for the same reasons that farmers combine into cooperatives. Not only does our government exempt unions and cooperatives from the charge of restraint of trade, but it has encouraged their growth as in the public interest.

Because the worker and the farmer lack effective bargaining power when they stand alone in the market place, Congress has prescribed minimum wages and provided farm price supports. The legislative branch of our government rightfully considers that the national welfare demands safeguards for both workers and farmers against the impact of "pure" competition.

Those who cry out against "labor monopolies" know these facts. They are well aware that the monopoly concept is not applicable to labor unions because unions do not suppress the competition that our society considers desirable.

They also know that in those few cases where unions do cooperate with employers to restrain competition in the sale of commodities, these cases are properly subject to the present antitrust laws.

The truth is that those who make the "labor monopoly" charge are not really concerned with competition or its negative counterpart, monopoly. Their real goal is the weakening of unions and especially those unions which they believe are too strong. . . .

The charge that labor unions are too strong is propaganda. No honest measure of the relative bargaining power of American employers and American unions will show that the strength of the unions is even equal to the strength of the employers.

Whether we measure the strength of unions and employers by their assets or by the results that they have been able to achieve, the comparison must show that there is no truth to the charge of overwhelming labor power.

It is obvious that the assets of even such a union as the United

Steelworkers of America cannot be compared with the assets of a single company like the United States Steel Corporation.

Nor do the results of economic bargains which have been made between American unions and employers support the charge of economic power. No responsible economist can claim that there has been an unjustly high distribution of wages to workers in recent years as against the distribution of profits to industry.

There are, of course, some few instances in which the strength of the union is greater than that of an individual employer. But this is usually countered by the development of employer associations which, incidentally, have not been charged with monopoly although their activities run far beyond collective bargaining.

One of the essentials of our free economic system is that we do not have government interference to redress every individual instance of economic imbalance so long as there is no general pattern of disequilibrium.

The real question behind the "labor-monopoly" charge is whether or not organized labor exercises too great an economic power for the public interest.

The only answer to this question is that America's unions do not have this excessive power. Our nation's industrial scene is not one in which poor, downtrodden, profitless business enterprises have lost every last penny to greedy labor unions.

Wage and profit statistics paint a contrary picture for our economy as a whole. In fact, these statistics show that only a minority of all our nation's wage earners are organized and many of these are organized in unions which cannot begin to match the economic power of their employers.

Even in those particular industries in which the large unions engage in company-wide bargaining, there is no data to support the charge that these unions have equal economic power with their opposite numbers at the bargaining table.

The "labor-monopoly" charge against American unions is false from every viewpoint. The "labor-monopoly" gimmick is no more than a different label on the old box of anti-union tactics still being peddled by the salesmen of reaction.

The Economics of Minimum-wage Legislation

GEORGE J. STIGLER

George J. Stigler, professor of economics at the University of Chicago, first published this provocative article in the American Economic Review *in June 1946.*

THE MINIMUM WAGE provisions of the Fair Labor Standards Act of 1938 have been repealed by inflation. Many voices are now taking up the cry for a higher minimum, say, of 60 to 75 cents per hour.

Economists have not been very outspoken on this type of legislation. It is my fundamental thesis that they can and should be outspoken, and singularly agreed. The popular objective of minimum wage legislation—the elimination of extreme poverty —is not seriously debatable. The important questions are rather (1) Does such legislation diminish poverty? (2) Are there efficient alternatives? The answers are, if I am not mistaken, unusually definite for questions of economic policy. If this is so, these answers should be given.

Some readers will probably know my answers already ("no" and "yes," respectively); it is distressing how often one can guess the answer given to an economic question merely by knowing who asks it. But my personal answers are unimportant; the arguments on which they rest, which are important, will be presented under four heads:
   1. Effects of a legal minimum wage on the allocation of resources.
   2. Effects on aggregate employment.
   3. Effects on family income.
   4. Alternative policies to combat poverty.

THE ALLOCATION OF RESOURCES

The effects of minimum wages may in principle differ between industries in which employers do and do not have control over the wage rates they pay for labor of given skill and application. The two possibilities will be discussed in turn.

Competitive Wage Determination · Each worker receives the value of his marginal product under competition. If a minimum wage is effective, it must therefore have one of two effects: first, workers whose services are worth less than the minimum wage are discharged (and thus forced into unregulated fields of employment, or into unemployment or retirement from the labor force); or, second, the productivity of low-efficiency workers is increased.

The former result, discharge of less efficient workers, will be larger the more the value of their services falls short of the legal minimum, the more elastic the demand for the product, and the greater the possibility of substituting other productive services (including efficient labor) for the inefficient workers' services. The discharged workers will, at best, move to unregulated jobs where they will secure lower returns. Unless inefficient workers' productivity rises, therefore, the minimum wage reduces aggregate output, perhaps raises the earnings of those previously a trifle below the minimum, and reduces the earnings of those substantially below the minimum. These are undoubtedly the main allocational effects of a minimum wage in a competitive industry.

The second and offsetting result, the increase of labor productivity, might come about in one of two ways: the laborers may work harder; or the entrepreneurs may use different production techniques. The threat of unemployment may force the inefficient laborers to work harder (the inducement of higher earnings had previously been available, and failed), but this is not very probable. These workers were already driven by the sharp spurs of poverty, and for many the intensity of effort must be increased beyond hope (up to 50 or more percent) to avoid discharge.

The introduction of new techniques by the entrepreneurs is the more common source of increased labor productivity. Here again there are two possibilities.

First, techniques which were previously unprofitable are now rendered profitable by the increased cost of labor. Costs of production rise because of the minimum wage, but they rise by less than they would if other resources could not be substituted for the labor. Employment will fall for two reasons: output falls; and a given output is secured with less labor. Commonly the new techniques require different (and hence superior) labor, so many inefficient workers are discharged. This process is only a spelling-out of the main competitive effect.

Second, entrepreneurs may be shocked out of lethargy to adopt techniques which were previously profitable or to discover new techniques. This "shock" theory is at present lacking in empirical evidence but not in popularity.

There are several reasons for believing that the "shock" theory is particularly inappropriate to the industries paying low wages. . . . A study of [the large manufacturing industry categories which in 1939 paid relatively low wages] suggests two generalizations: (1) the low-wage industries are competitive, and (2) the ratio of wages to total-processing-cost-plus-profit is higher than in high-wage industries. The competitive nature of these industries argues that the entrepreneurs are not easy-going traditionalists: vigorous competition in national markets does not attract or tolerate such men. The relatively high labor costs reveal that inducements to wage-economy are already strong. These considerations both work strongly against the shock theory in low-wage manufacturing industries in 1939. Since these industries were on the whole much less affected by the war than other manufacturing industries, they will probably be present in the post-war list of low-wage industries. The low-wage industries in trade and services display the same characteristics and support the same adverse conclusion with respect to the shock theory.

Employer Wage Determination · If an employer has a significant degree of control over the wage rate he pays for a given quality of labor, a skillfully-set minimum wage may increase his employment and wage rate and, because the wage is brought closer to the value of the marginal product, at the same time increase aggregate output. The effect may be elucidated with the hypothetical data in the table above. If the entrepreneur is left alone, he will set a wage of $20 and employ 50 men; a minimum wage of $24 will increase employment to 70 men.

This arithmetic is quite valid, but it is not very relevant to the question of a national minimum wage. The minimum wage

Hypothetical Data Illustrating Employer Wage Determination

Number of workers	Wage rate	Marginal cost of a worker	Value of the marginal product [*]
10	$12		$36
20	14	$16	34
30	16	20	32
40	18	24	30
50	20	28	28
60	22	32	26
70	24	36	24

[*] Or marginal value product, if this is less.

which achieves these desirable ends has several requisites:

1. It must be chosen correctly: too high a wage (over $28 in our example) will decrease employment. The accounting records describe, very imperfectly, existing employment and wages; the optimum minimum wage can be set only if the demand and supply schedules are known over a considerable range. At present there is no tolerably accurate method of deriving these schedules, and one is entitled to doubt that a legislative mandate is all that is necessary to bring forth such a method.
2. The optimum wage varies with occupation (and, within an occupation, with the quality of worker).
3. The optimum wage varies among firms (and plants).
4. The optimum wage varies, often rapidly, through time.

A uniform national minimum wage, infrequently changed, is wholly unsuited to these diversities of conditions.[1]

We may sum up: the legal minimum wage will reduce aggregate output, and it will decrease the earnings of workers who had previously been receiving materially less than the minimum.

AGGREGATE EMPLOYMENT

Although no precise estimate of the effects of a minimum wage upon aggregate employment is possible, we may nevertheless form some notion of the direction of these effects. The higher the minimum wage, the greater will be the number of covered

1. One can go much farther: even administratively established minima, varying with firm and time, would be impossibly difficult to devise and revise, and their effects on private investment would be extremely adverse.

workers who are discharged. The current proposals would probably affect a twentieth to a tenth of all covered workers, so possibly several hundred thousand workers would be discharged. Whatever the number (which no one knows), the direct unemployment is substantial and certain; and it fairly establishes the presumption that the net effects of the minimum wage on aggregate employment are adverse.

This presumption is strengthened by the existing state of aggregate money demand. There is no prospective inadequacy of money demand in the next year or two—indeed, the danger is that it is excessive. If the minimum wage were to increase the relative share of wage-earners and, hence, the propensity to consume—which requires the uncertain assumption that the demand for inefficient labor is inelastic—the increment of consumer demand will be unnecessary, and perhaps unwelcome. (Conversely, the direct unemployment resulting from the wage law would diminish faster in a period of high employment.)

It is sufficient for the present argument that no large increase in employment will be induced by the legislation. Actually, there is a presumption that a minimum wage will have adverse effects upon aggregate employment.

WAGE RATES AND FAMILY INCOME

The manipulation of individual prices is neither an efficient nor an equitable device for changing the distribution of personal income. This is a well-known dictum that has received much documentation in analyses of our agricultural programs. The relevance of the dictum to minimum wage legislation is easily demonstrated.

One cannot expect a close relationship between the level of hourly wage rates and the amount of family income. Yet family income and needs are the fundamental factors in the problem of poverty. The major sources of discrepancy may be catalogued.

First, the hourly rates are effective only for those who receive them, and it was shown in Section 1 that the least productive workers are forced into uncovered occupations or into unemployment.

Second, hourly earnings and annual earnings are not closely related. The seasonality of the industry, the extent of overtime, the amount of absenteeism, and the shift of workers among industries, are obvious examples of factors which reduce the correlation between hourly earnings and annual earnings.

Third, family earnings are the sum of earnings of all workers in the family, and the dispersion of number of workers is considerable. . . .

Fourth, although wages are, of course, the chief component of the income of low-wage families, they are by no means the only component. . . .

All of these steps lead us only to family income; the leap must still be made to family needs. It is argued in the next section that family composition is the best criterion of need, and whether this be accepted or not, it is clearly an important criterion.

The connection between hourly wages and the standard of living of the family is thus remote and fuzzy. Unless the minimum wage varies with the amount of employment, number of earners, non-wage income, family size, and many other factors, it will be an inept device for combatting poverty even for those who succeed in retaining employment. And if the minimum wage varies with all of these factors, it will be an insane device.

THE PROBLEM OF POVERTY

Minimum wage legislation commonly has two stated objectives: the reduction of employer control of wages and the abolition of poverty. The former and much lesser purpose may better be achieved by removing the condition of labor immobility which gives rise to employer control. Labor immobility would be reduced substantially by public provision of comprehensive information on employment conditions in various areas and industries. The immobility would be further reduced by supplying vocational training and loans to cover moving costs. But employer wage control is not the important problem; let us turn to the elimination of poverty.

Incomes of the poor cannot be increased without impairing incentives. Skillful policies will, for a given increase in the incomes of the poor, impair incentives less than clumsy policies. But the more completely poverty is eliminated, given the level of intelligence with which this is done, the greater will be the impairment of incentives. This is a price we must pay, just as impairment of incentives is a price we have willingly paid to reduce the inequality of income by progressive income and estate taxes. Society must determine, through its legislators, what minimum income (or addition to income) should be guaranteed to each family. We shall assume that this difficult decision has been made.

One principle is fundamental in the amelioration of poverty: those who are equally in need should be helped equally. If this principle is to be achieved, there must be an objective criterion of need; equality can never be achieved when many cases are judged (by many people) "on their merits." We are driven almost inexorably to family size and composition as this criterion of need. It is obviously imperfect; the sickly require more medical care than the healthy.[2] But it is vastly easier to accord special treatment to certain families for a few items like medical care than to accord special treatment to every family for the sum of all items of expenditure.

It is a corollary of this position that assistance should not be based upon occupation. The poor farmer, the poor shopkeeper, and the poor miner are on an equal footing. There may be administrative justification (although I doubt it) for treating the farmer separately from the urban dweller, but there is no defense in equity for helping the one and neglecting the other. To render the assistance by manipulating prices is in any case objectionable: we help the rich farmer more than the poor, and give widely differing amounts of help to the poor farmer from year to year.

The principle of equity thus involves the granting of assistance to the poor with regard to their need (measured by family composition) but without regard to their occupation. There is a possible choice between grants in kind and in money. The latter commends itself strongly: it gives full play to the enormous variety of tastes and it is administratively much simpler. Yet it raises a problem which will be noticed shortly.

Even if these general observations be accepted, the structure

2. One could argue that rural families should receive less help, to offset the lower prices at which food and housing are procured. The group is of sufficient size and perhaps sufficiently identifiable to justify separate treatment. But there are grounds other than political expediency for rejecting this proposal.

of administration is of grave importance, and I do not pretend to have explored this field. There is great attractiveness in the proposal that we extend the personal income tax to the lowest income brackets with negative rates in these brackets. Such a scheme could achieve equality of treatment with what appears to be a (large) minimum of administrative machinery. If the negative rates are appropriately graduated, we may still retain some measure of incentive for a family to increase its income. We should no doubt encounter many perplexing difficulties in carrying out this plan, but they are problems which could not be avoided, even though they might be ignored, by a less direct attack on poverty.

One final point: We seek to abolish poverty in good part because it leads to undernourishment. In this connection, dietary appraisals show that in any income class, no matter how low, a portion of the families secure adequate diets, and in any income class, as high as the studies go, a portion do not. The proportion of ill-fed, to be sure, declines substantially as income rises, but it does not disappear. We cannot possibly afford to abolish malnutrition, or mal-housing, or mal-education, only by increasing incomes.

Either of two inferences may be drawn. The program of increasing income must be supplemented by a program of education—in diet, in housing, in education! Or the assistance to the poor should be given in kind, expertly chosen. The latter approach is administratively very complex, but quicker and in direct expenditure vastly more economical. These factors affect our choice, but a thought should be given also to the two societies to which they lead.

Minimum-wage Legislation: Another View

FRED H. BLUM

In this essay Fred H. Blum replies to Professor Stigler's criticisms of minimum-wage legislation.

PROFESSOR STIGLER'S DISCUSSION "The Economics of Minimum-wage Legislation" is not intended to be an exercise in pure economics but an answer to the "many voices [who] are now taking up the cry for a higher minimum, say of 60 to 75 cents per hour."

Professor Stigler's criticism of the proposed increase of minimum wage rates of 40 to 65 cents per hour is expressed in two propositions: (1) that statutory minimum wages are an inadequate means of eliminating poverty—which he considers the main objective of minimum wage legislation and of eliminating employer's control over wages—which he considers to be its secondary aim, and (2) that there are alternative means better suited to achieve these objectives.

Professor Stigler gives the following reasons for the inadequacy of minimum wages to eliminate poverty: (1) because the connection between hourly wages and the standard of living . . . is "remote and fuzzy" and (2) because minimum wage legislation will lead to a decline in employment.

It is true that the hourly rate is not the only factor influencing the standard of living. But the wage rate and the volume of employment are the two most important elements determining the worker's income. A criticism of minimum wage legislation for putting a floor under the hourly and not the annual income is therefore not valid. Such a criticism is based, furthermore, on a wrong conception of the real objectives of minimum wage legislation.

This writer is not aware of anyone who had advocated minimum wages as a means of eliminating poverty as such. It seems more appropriate to state that the objectives of the minimum wage legislation are (1) to eliminate that part of poverty which is caused by the existence of wage rates which do not allow workers sufficient earnings to have a minimum standard of living *even if employment were continuous*, (2) to eliminate unfair competition based on substandard wage rates, and (3) to increase mass purchasing power. Minimum wage legislation is not intended to be limited to cases in which the employer has control over wages.[1]

Given these objectives, the real issue is whether minimum wages can contribute to the elimination of poverty in the way the Fair Labor Standards Act (FLSA) has intended. To answer this question we have to examine the effect of minimum wages on employment—the second main determinant of the standard of living.

Professor Stigler believes that the increase in hourly wages will detrimentally affect the volume of employment. Minimum wages, according to him, will decrease employment (1) by reduction in output, (2) by discharge of workers whose productivity cannot be increased, and (3) by technological improvements which reduce the labor requirements per unit of output. The net result will be a decrease in the earnings of workers who had "previously been receiving materially less than the minimum" and "perhaps a rise" of the earnings of those "previously a trifle below the minimum."

The experience which resulted from the FLSA showed that minimum wages did not increase costs to such an extent as to affect the demand for commodities. Case studies in which the impact of minimum wages could be isolated from other factors affecting production, employment, and earnings have shown that employment did not decrease because of changes in demand and output. But it had a tendency to decrease because of technological improvements. In spite of this tendency, earnings of workers previously receiving less than the minimum wage increased substantially, and earnings of those previously above the minimum wage increased also, though to a smaller extent.

1. The need for minimum wage legislation often exists in cases in which employers have no control over wages. There were few monopsonistic employers in the city of New York but there were widespread labor conditions detrimental to the maintenance of a minimum standard of living. These conditions caused unfair competition in the very cases in which competition was unimpeded.

This seems to show that Professor Stigler's conclusions in regard to earnings and output are incorrect, but that his conclusions in regard to the employment effects are partially right. In determining to what extent they are correct, we must distinguish clearly between the displacement of labor due to increased productivity and the displacement resulting from the inability of the worker to increase his productivity up to the point where it would be equal to the value of his marginal product. It is one thing to point out that minimum wages increase productivity; it is another to criticize the effectiveness of minimum wages to contribute to an elimination of poverty because they lead to dismissal of workers with substandard productivity.

In so far as Professor Stigler has the latter phenomenon in mind, he is wrong. The experience of the FLSA has shown that the productivity of submarginal workers has increased.[2] It is true that there were some handicapped workers whose productivity could not be increased. They were not dismissed but certified as handicapped. In so far as Professor Stigler thinks in terms of technological unemployment his reasoning is correct but meaningless. His criticism of minimum wages for having a tendency to reduce labor requirements per unit of output is tantamount to a criticism of minimum wage legislation for contributing to economic progress, an increased standard of living, and higher income.[3]

The remoteness of Professor Stigler's conclusion from the experience made with the FLSA becomes understandable if we realize that he did not investigate any empirical material. His conclusions are deduced from the following premises: (1) that "each worker receives the value of his marginal product"; (2)

2. Minimum wage legislation led to a general re-examination of labor policies with the objective of increasing efficiency. Improvement of employment techniques followed. Pretraining of employees, vocational schools and attention to lighting were some of the results of minimum wage legislation. See H. M. Douty, "Minimum Wage Regulations in the Seamless Hosiery Industry," *Southern Economic Journal*, October, 1961, esp. p. 147, and John F. Maloney, "Some Effects of the Federal Fair Labor Standards Act upon Southern Industry," *Southern Economic Journal*, July, 1942, pp. 19–20.

3. It is true that the latter results are only potential and do not follow necessarily from increases in productivity if the dynamic forces giving life to our economy are not strong enough to absorb technological unemployment. But this is a problem of a different nature which cannot be solved by stopping technological progress.

that there is perfect competition in a static equilibrium society; (3) that both the product market and the labor market are perfectly competitive.[4] Only when discussing employer's control over wages does Professor Stigler make a concession to the real world.[5] But the main trend of his paper is based on assumptions which are irreconcilable with the objectives of the FLSA and the economic realities within which it operates.

The conclusions at which Professor Stigler arrived on the basis of these assumptions are used to predict that "possibly several hundred thousand workers would be discharged" if the current proposals to amend the FLSA were put into effect.[6] In addition to warning us against mass unemployment, Professor Stigler states that "the increment of consumer demand (resulting from an increase in the relative share of wage earners' income

4. It is true that in his reasoning Professor Stigler fails to distinguish between perfect competition in a classical model of *laissez-faire* theory in which unemployment does not exist and in the real world in which unemployment always exists. But in stipulating equality of wages and marginal product of labor, Professor Stigler must accept the neoclassical assumptions mentioned above. His assumption that wage determination is competitive because "low wage industries are competitive" is only meaningful in the ideal world of *laissez faire*. In the real world a competitive product market often involves labor conditions detrimental to the maintenance of a minimum standard of living.

5. Professor Stigler points out that "in such a case a minimum wage may be beneficial" because the wage is brought closer to the value of the marginal product. This shows that his assumption of equality of wages and the value of the marginal product of labor loses even its theoretical meaning if there is so substantial an element of monopoly as there is in the real world.

6. Empirical evidence shows that this prediction is wrong—even if we accept Professor Stigler's assumptions. In manufacturing, for which we have the best data, 2.3 million workers received less than 65 cents an hour in June, 1945. The overall straight time hourly wage rate would have increased 2 percent (from $0.968 to $0.987) as a result of the proposed increase of the statutory minimum wage from 40 to 65 cents per hour. The additional cost to the wage bill would have corresponded to 3.5 percent of 1944 profits. Mr. Bowles testified to the Senate Committee on Education and Labor that only one industry—the lumber industry—would need price relief as a consequence of the proposed increase in the minimum wage. We may mention in addition that the suggested relative increases in the statutory minimum wage are not greater than those enacted in 1938 when anything but mass unemployment resulted from the enactment of the FLSA. See "Basic Data on Workers in Manufacturing below 65 cents Minimum and Effect of 65 Cents Minimum," Hearings on S. 1349, pp. 1423, 1428, and 1439 ff. It should be pointed out that these estimates take into consideration only the direct effect of an increase in the statutory minimum wage.

due to a minimum wage) will be unnecessary, and perhaps unwelcome."

We shall not discuss the question whether it would be unwelcome to increase the income of families presently earning $800 per year or whether other anti-inflation measures are socially more desirable. But we must point out that Professor Stigler's argument is meaningful only if we assume that large-scale increases in purchasing power result from minimum wage legislation. To postulate such a consequence is completely incompatible with Professor Stigler's dire prediction of mass unemployment.

We have thus far reviewed Professor Stigler's arguments in terms of the efficacy of minimum wages to achieve certain objectives. We have seen that his arguments are largely irrelevant since he ignores the actual objective and the effects of the FLSA as well as the economic realities within which it operates. We have seen, furthermore, that he does not prove his case even in terms of his own interpretation of the objectives of the FLSA. But final judgment as to the validity of Professor Stigler's reasoning is not possible before discussing the alternatives he proposed.

The proposals made by Professor Stigler are twofold: (1) elimination of immobility of labor, (2) "assistance to the poor with regard to their need (measured by family composition) but without regard to their occupation." It is not clear how immobility of labor is compatible with Professor Stigler's assumption. But it undoubtedly exists in the real world and any policy which decreases the immobility of labor is welcome. But it is certain that the measures proposed by Mr. Stigler to eliminate immobility of labor would be inadequate. They could, at best, be a partial substitute for minimum wage legislation—or a valuable complementary measure.

Negative rates for personal income taxes for low-income families are the second alternative proposed by Professor Stigler. This is neither an "efficient" nor an "equitable" means of eliminating poverty because if applied as an alternative rather than as a complementary measure to minimum wage legislation, it would be nothing but a public subsidy for unfair competition and/or monopsonistic exploitation. It would in no way eliminate labor conditions detrimental to the maintenance of a minimum standard of living and would therefore not be a real alternative to minimum wage legislation.

Professor Stigler's advocacy of his alternatives and his rejection of minimum wage legislation as "neither a sufficient nor equitable device for changing the distribution of personal income" brings out an important point. There is at least a presumption that Professor Stigler's concept of equity is different from that implicit in minimum wage legislation. Professor Stigler essentially advocates doles based on the means test. He seeks to abolish poverty "in good part because it leads to undernourishment." And he believes that the "incomes of the poor cannot be raised without impairing incentives." We may remark in passing that there is no explanation why tax rebates would not bring about the same results—nor why they are not inflationary. The main point is that the advocates of statutory minimum wages would probably feel that a democratic society implies a different concept of equity and human dignity and therefore different means of implementation.

This shows that a social scientist who criticizes a specific measure of economic policy should clearly differentiate between the ability of a proposed measure to achieve the desired aim and the desirability of the aim itself. It is true that Professor Stigler says he approves of the elimination of "extreme poverty." But such a statement is far too vague; it is not a clear enough indication of the value judgments in regard to means and ends implicit in his reasoning. In order to make these value judgments explicit a scientist must show the implications of a specific measure of policy, the "price" that we must pay for it, and he must indicate the "price" of alternative policies. This can only be done by taking the existing society as a *frame of reference* and by indicating the *norm* in view of which social criticism is made. It seems that Professor Stigler is taking the world of perfect competition in which wages are equal to the marginal product as a frame of reference as well as a norm for judging the impact of minimum wage legislation. A criticism of minimum wage legislation from this point of view is meaningless. If the world of perfect competition is taken as a concrete frame of reference, minimum wages cease to be a problem and the objectives of minimum wage legislation become unreal. If the world of perfect competition is taken as a norm, the criticism becomes merely formal, devoid of any reality and must lose even the pretense of social significance.

PART THREE

Labor Problems of Minorities
and Women

On Improving the Economic Status
of the Negro

JAMES TOBIN

*James Tobin, author of this widely cited discussion of the un-
equal status of black workers, is professor of economics at Yale
University.*

I START from the presumption that the integration of Negroes into
the American society and economy can be accomplished within
existing political and economic institutions. I understand the im-
patience of those who think otherwise, but I see nothing in-
compatible between our peculiar mixture of private enterprise
and government, on the one hand, and the liberation and integration of the Negro, on the other. Indeed the present position
of the Negro is an aberration from the principles of our society,
rather than a requirement of its functioning. Therefore, my suggestions are directed to the aim of mobilizing existing powers
of government to bring Negroes into full participation in the
mainstream of American economic life.

The economic plight of individuals, Negroes and whites alike,
can always be attributed to specific handicaps and circumstances:
discrimination, immobility, lack of education and experience, ill
health, weak motivation, poor neighborhood, large family size,
burdensome family responsibilities. Such diagnoses suggest a
host of specific remedies, some in the domain of civil rights,
others in the war on poverty. Important as these remedies are,
there is a danger that the diagnoses are myopic. They explain
why certain individuals rather than others suffer from the
economic maladies of the time. They do not explain why the
overall incidence of the maladies varies dramatically from time

63

to time—for example, why personal attributes which seemed to doom a man to unemployment in 1932 or even in 1954 or 1961 did not so handicap him in 1944 or 1951 or 1956.

Public health measures to improve the environment are often more productive in conquering disease than a succession of individual treatments. Malaria was conquered by oiling and draining swamps, not by quinine. The analogy holds for economic maladies. Unless the global incidence of these misfortunes can be diminished, every indivdual problem successfully solved will be replaced by a similar problem somewhere else. That is why an economist is led to emphasize the importance of the overall economic climate.

Over the decades, general economic progress has been the major factor in the gradual conquest of poverty. Recently some observers, J. K. Galbraith and Michael Harrington most eloquently, have contended that this process no longer operates. The economy may prosper and labor may become steadily more productive as in the past, but "the other America" will be stranded. Prosperity and progress have already eliminated almost all the easy cases of poverty, leaving a hard core beyond the reach of national economic trends. There may be something to the "backwash" thesis as far as whites are concerned. But it definitely does not apply to Negroes. Too many of them are poor. It cannot be true that half of a race of twenty million human beings are victims of specific disabilities which insulate them from the national economic climate. It cannot be true, and it is not. Locke Anderson has shown that the pace of Negro economic progress is peculiarly sensitive to general economic growth. He estimates that if nationwide per capita personal income is stationary, nonwhite median family income falls by 0.5 percent per year, while if national per capita income grows 5 percent, nonwhite income grows nearly 7.5 percent.

National prosperity and economic growth are still powerful engines for improving the economic status of Negroes. They are not doing enough and they are not doing it fast enough. There is ample room for a focused attack on the specific sources of Negro poverty. But a favorable overall economic climate is a necessary condition for the global success—as distinguished from success in individual cases—of specific efforts to remedy the handicaps associated with Negro poverty.

THE IMPORTANCE OF A TIGHT LABOR MARKET

. . . The magnitude of America's poverty problem already reflects the failure of the economy in the second postwar decade
to match its performance in the first. Had the 1947–56 rate of
growth of median family income been maintained since 1957,
and had unemployment been steadily limited to 4 percent, it is
estimated that the fraction of the population with poverty incomes in 1963 would have been 16.6 percent instead of 18.5 percent. The educational qualifications of the labor force have
continued to improve. The principle of racial equality, in employment as in other activities, has gained ground both in law
and in the national conscience. If, despite all this, dropouts,
inequalities in educational attainment, and discrimination in
employment seem more serious today rather than less, the
reason is that the overall economic climate has not been favorable
after all.

The most important dimension of the overall economic climate
is the tightness of the labor market. In a tight labor market unemployment is low and short in duration, and job vacancies are
plentiful. People who stand at the end of the hiring line and the
top of the layoff list have the most to gain from a tight labor
market. It is not surprising that the position of Negroes relative
to that of whites improves in a tight labor market and declines in
a slack market. Unemployment itself is only one way in which a
slack labor market hurts Negroes and other disadvantaged
groups, and the gains from reduction in unemployment are by
no means confined to the employment of persons counted as
unemployed. A tight labor market means not just jobs, but better
jobs, longer hours, higher wages. Because of the heavy demands
for labor during the Second World War and its economic after-
math, Negroes made dramatic relative gains between 1940 and
1950. Unfortunately this momentum has not been maintained,
and the blame falls largely on the weakness of labor markets
since 1957.

The shortage of jobs has hit Negro men particularly hard and
thus has contributed mightily to the ordeal of the Negro family,
which is in turn the cumulative source of so many other social
disorders. The unemployment rate of Negro men is more sensitive than that of Negro women to the national rate. Since 1949

Negro women have gained in median income relative to white women, but Negro men have lost ground to white males. In a society which stresses breadwinning as the expected role of the mature male and occupational achievement as his proper goal, failure to find and to keep work is devastating to the man's self-respect and family status. Matriarchy is in any case a strong tradition in Negro society, and the man's role is further downgraded when the family must and can depend on the woman for its livelihood. It is very important to increase the proportion of Negro children who grow up in stable families with two parents. Without a strong labor market it will be extremely difficult to do so.

Unemployment · It is well known that Negro unemployment rates are multiples of the general unemployment rate. This fact reflects both the lesser skills, seniority, and experience of Negroes and employers' discrimination against Negroes. These conditions are a deplorable reflection on American society, but as long as they exist Negroes suffer much more than others from a general increase in unemployment and gain much more from a general reduction. A rule of thumb is that changes in the nonwhite unemployment rate are twice those in the white rate. The rule works both ways. Nonwhite unemployment went from 4.1 percent in 1953, a tight labor market year, to 12.5 percent in 1961, while the white rate rose from 2.3 percent to 6 percent. By 1965 the Negro rate had declined by 2.4 percent, the white rate by 1.2 from the 1961 levels.

Even the Negro teenage unemployment rate shows some sensitivity to general economic conditions. Recession increased it from 15 percent in 1955–56 to 25 percent in 1958. It decreased to 22 percent in 1960 but rose to 28 percent in 1963. Teenage unemployment is abnormally high now, relative to that of other age groups, because the wave of postwar babies is coming into the labor market. Most of them, especially the Negroes, are crowding the end of the hiring line. But their prospects for getting jobs are no less dependent on general labor market conditions.

Part-time Work · Persons who are involuntarily forced to work part time instead of full time are not counted as unemployed, but their number goes up and down with the unemployment rate. Just as Negroes bear a disproportionate share of unemployment, they bear more than their share of involuntary part-time unemployment. A tight labor market will not only employ more Negroes; it will also give more of those who are employed full-time jobs. In both respects, it will reduce disparities between whites and Negroes.

Labor-force Participation · In a tight market, of which a low unemployment rate is a barometer, the labor force itself is larger. Job opportunities draw into the labor force individuals who, simply because the prospects were dim, did not previously regard themselves as seeking work and were therefore not enumerated as unemployed. For the economy as a whole, it appears that an expansion of job opportunities enough to reduce unemployment by one worker will bring another worker into the labor force.

This phenomenon is important for many Negro families. Statistically, their poverty now appears to be due more often to the lack of a breadwinner in the labor force than to unemployment. But in a tight labor market many members of these families, including families now on public assistance, would be drawn into employment. Labor-force participation rates are roughly 2 percent lower for nonwhite men than for white men, and the disparity increases in years of slack labor markets. The story is different for women. Negro women have always been in the labor force to a much greater extent than white women. A real improvement in the economic status of Negro men and in the stability of Negro families would probably lead to a reduction in labor-force participation by Negro women. But for teenagers, participation rates for Negroes are not so high as for whites; and for women twenty to twenty-four they are about the same. These relatively low rates are undoubtedly due less to voluntary choice than to the same lack of job opoprtunities that produces phenomenally high unemployment rates for young Negro women.

Duration of Unemployment · In a tight labor market, such unemployment as does exist is likely to be of short duration. Short-term unemployment is less damaging to the economic welfare of the unemployed. More will have earned and fewer will have exhausted private and public unemployment benefits. In 1953 when the overall unemployment rate was 2.9 percent, only 4 percent of the unemployed were out of work for longer than twenty-six weeks and only 11 percent for longer than fifteen weeks. In contrast, the unemployment rate in 1961 was 6.7 percent; and of the unemployed in that year, 17 percent were out of work for longer than twenty-six weeks and 32 percent for longer than fifteen weeks. Between the first quarter of 1964 and the first quarter of 1965, overall unemployment fell 11 percent, while unemployment extending beyond half a year was lowered by 22 percent.

As Rashi Fein points out elsewhere in this volume [pp. 83–105], one more dimension of society's inequity to the Negro is that an unemployed Negro is more likely to stay unemployed than an unemployed white. But his figures also show that Negroes share in the reduction of long-term unemployment accompanying economic expansion.

Migration from Agriculture · A tight labor market draws the surplus rural population to higher paying nonagricultural jobs. Southern Negroes are a large part of this surplus rural population. Migration is the only hope for improving their lot, or their children's. In spite of the vast migration of past decades, there are still about 775,000 Negroes, 11 percent of the Negro labor force of the country, who depend on the land for their living and that of their families. Almost a half million live in the South, and almost all of them are poor.

Migration from agriculture and from the South is the Negroes' historic path toward economic improvement and equality. It is a smooth path for Negroes and for the urban communities to which they move only if there is a strong demand for labor in towns and cities North and South. In the 1940s the number of Negro farmers and farm laborers in the nation fell by 450,000 and 1.5 million Negroes (net) left the South. This was the great decade of Negro economic advance. In the 1950s the same occupational and geographical migration continued undiminished. The movement to higher-income occupations and locations should have raised the relative economic status of Negroes. But in the 1950s Negroes were moving into increasingly weak job markets. Too often disguised unemployment in the countryside was simply transformed into enumerated unemployment, and rural poverty into urban poverty.

Quality of Jobs · In a slack labor market, employers can pick and choose, both in recruiting and in promoting. They exaggerate the skill, education, and experience requirements of their jobs. They use diplomas, or color, or personal histories as convenient screening devices. In a tight market, they are forced to be realistic, to tailor job specifications to the available supply, and to give on-the-job training. They recruit and train applicants whom they would otherwise screen out, and they upgrade employees whom they would in slack times consign to low-wage, low-skill, and part-time jobs.

Wartime and other experience shows that job requirements are adjustable and that men and women are trainable. It is only in slack times that people worry about a mismatch between supposedly rigid occupational requirements and supposedly unchangeable qualifications of the labor force. As already noted, the relative status of Negroes improves in a tight labor market not only in respect to unemployment, but also in respect to wages and occupations.

Cyclical Fluctuation · Sustaining a high demand for labor is important. The in-and-out status of the Negro in the business cycle damages his long-term position because periodic unemployment robs him of experience and seniority.

Restrictive Practices. A slack labor market probably accentuates the discriminatory and protectionist proclivities of certain crafts and unions. When jobs are scarce, opening the door to Negroes is a real threat. Of course prosperity will not automatically dissolve the barriers, but it will make it more difficult to oppose efforts to do so.

I conclude that the single most important step the nation could take to improve the economic position of the Negro is to operate the economy steadily at a low rate of unemployment. We cannot expect to restore the labor market conditions of the Second World War, and we do not need to. In the years 1951–1953, unemployment was roughly 3 percent, teenage unemployment around 7 percent, Negro unemployment about 4.5 percent, long term unemployment negligible. In the years 1955–57, general unemployment was roughly 4 percent, and the other measures correspondingly higher. Four percent is the official target of the Kennedy-Johnson Administration. It has not been achieved since 1957. Reaching and maintaining 4 percent would be a tremendous improvement over the performance of the last eight years. But we should not stop there; the society and the Negro can benefit immensely from tightening the labor market still further, to 3.5 or 3 percent unemployment. The administration itself has never defined 4 percent as anything other than an "interim" target.

WHY DON'T WE HAVE A TIGHT LABOR MARKET?

We know how to operate the economy so that there is a tight labor market. By fiscal and monetary measures the federal government can control aggregate spending in the economy. The government could choose to control it so that unemployment averaged 3.5 or 3 percent instead of remaining over 4.5 percent except at occasional business cycle peaks. Moreover, recent experience here and abroad shows that we can probably narrow the amplitude of fluctuations around whatever average we select as a target.

Some observers have cynically concluded that a society like ours can achieve full employment only in wartime. But aside from conscription into the armed services, government action creates jobs in wartime by exactly the same mechanism as in peacetime—the government spends more money and stimulates private firms and citizens to spend more too. It is the amount of spending, not its purpose, that does the trick. Public or private spending to go to the moon, build schools, or conquer poverty can be just as effective in reducing unemployment as spending to build airplanes and submarines—if there is enough of it. There may be more political constraints and ideological inhibitions in peacetime, but the same techniques of economic policy are available if we want badly enough to use them. The two main reasons we do not take this relatively simple way out are two obsessive fears, inflation and balance of payments deficits.

Running the economy with a tight labor market would mean a somewhat faster upward creep in the price level. The disadvantages of this are, in my view, exaggerated and are scarcely commensurable with the real economic and social gains of higher output and employment. Moreover, there are ways of protecting "widows and orphans" against erosion in the purchasing power of their savings. But fear of inflation is strong both in the U.S. financial establishment and in the public at large. The vast comfortable white middle class who are never touched by unemployment prefer to safeguard the purchasing power of their life insurance and pension rights than to expand opportunities for the disadvantaged and unemployed.

The fear of inflation would operate anyway, but it is accentuated by U.S. difficulties with its international balance of payments. These difficulties have seriously constrained and hampered U.S. fiscal and monetary policy in recent years. Any rise in prices might enlarge the deficit. An aggressively expansionary monetary policy, lowering interest rates, might push money out of the country.

In the final analysis what we fear is that we might not be able to defend the parity of the dollar with gold, that is, to sell gold at $35 an ounce to any government that wants to buy. So great is the gold mystique that this objective has come to occupy a niche in the hierarchy of U.S. goals second only to the military defense of the country, and not always to that. It is not fanciful to link the plight of Negro teenagers in Harlem to the monetary whims of General de Gaulle. But it is only our own attachment to "the dollar" as an abstraction which makes us cringe before the European appetite for gold.

This topic is too charged with technical complexities, real and imagined, and with confused emotions to be discussed adequately here. I will confine myself to three points. First, the United States is the last country in the world which needs to hold back its own economy to balance its international accounts. To let the tail wag the dog is not in the interests of the rest of the world, so much of which depends on us for trade and capital, any more than in our own.

Second, forces are at work to restore balance to American international accounts—the increased competitiveness of our exports and the income from the large investments our firms and citizens have made overeas since the war. Meanwhile we can finance deficits by gold reserves and lines of credit at the International Monetary Fund and at foreign central banks. Ultimately we have one foolproof line of defense—letting the dollar depreciate relative to foreign currencies. The world would not end. The sun would rise the next day. American products would be more competitive in world markets. Neither God nor the Constitution fixed the gold value of the dollar. The U.S. would not be the first country to let its currency depreciate. Nor would it be the first time for the U.S.—not until we stopped "saving" the dollar and the gold standard in 1933 did our recovery from the Great Depression begin.

Third, those who oppose taking such risks argue that the dollar today occupies a unique position as international money, that the world as a whole has an interest, which we cannot ignore, in the stability of the gold value of the dollar. If so, we can reasonably ask the rest of the world, especially our European friends, to share the burdens which guaranteeing this stability imposes upon us.

This has been an excursion into general economic policy. But the connection between gold and the plight of the Negro is no less real for being subtle. We are paying much too high a social price for avoiding creeping inflation and for protecting our gold stock and "the dollar." But it will not be easy to alter these national priorities. The interests of the unemployed, the poor, and the Negroes are underrepresented in the comfortable consensus which supports and confines current policy.

Another approach, which can be pursued simultaneously, is to diminish the conflicts among these competing objectives, in particular to reduce the degree of inflation associated with low levels of unemployment. This can be done in two ways. One way is to improve the mobility of labor and other resources to occupations, locations, and industries where bottlenecks would otherwise lead to wage and price increases. This is where many specific programs, such as the training and retraining of manpower and policies to improve the technical functioning of labor markets, come into their own.

A second task is to break down the barriers to competition which now restrict the entry of labor and enterprise into certain occupations and industries. These lead to wage- and price-increasing bottlenecks even when resources are not really short. Many barriers are created by public policy itself, in response to the vested interests concerned. Many reflect concentration of economic power in unions and in industry. These barriers represent another way in which the advantaged and the employed purchase their standards of living and their security at the expense of unprivileged minorities.

In the best of circumstances, structural reforms of these kinds will be slow and gradual. They will encounter determined economic and political resistance from special interests which are powerful in Congress and state legislatures. Moreover, Congressmen and legislators represent places rather than people and are likely to oppose, not facilitate, the increased geographical mobility which is required. It is no accident that our manpower programs do not include relocation allowances.

INCREASING THE EARNING CAPACITY OF NEGROES

Given the proper overall economic climate, in particular a steadily tight labor market, the Negro's economic condition can be expected to improve, indeed to improve dramatically. But not fast enough. Not as fast as his aspirations or as the aspirations he has taught the rest of us to have for him. What else can be done? I shall confine myself to a few comments and suggestions that occur to a general economist.

Even in a tight labor market, the Negro's relative status will suffer both from current discrimination and from his lower earning capacity, the result of inferior acquired skill. In a real sense both factors reflect discrimination, since the Negro's handicaps in earning capacity are the residue of decades of discrimination in education and employment. Nevertheless for both analysis and policy it is useful to distinguish the two.

Discrimination means that the Negro is denied access to certain markets where he might sell his labor, and to certain markets where he might purchase goods and services. Elementary application of "supply and demand" makes it clear that these restrictions are bound to result in his selling his labor for less and buying his livelihood for more than if these barriers did not exist. If Negro women can be clerks only in certain stores, those storekeepers will not need to pay them so much as they pay whites. If Negroes can live only in certain houses, the prices and rents they have to pay will be high for the quality of accommodation provided.

Successful elimination of discrimination is not only important in itself but will also have substantial economic benefits. Since residential segregation is the key to so much else and so difficult to eliminate by legal fiat alone, the power of the purse should be unstintingly used. I see no reason that the expenditure of funds for this purpose should be confined to new construction. Why not establish private or semipublic revolving funds to purchase, for resale or rental on a desegregated basis, strategically located existing structures as they become available?

The effects of past discrimination will take much longer to eradicate. The sins against the fathers are visited on the children. They are deprived of the intellectual and social capital which in our society is supposed to be transmitted in the family and the home. We have only begun to realize how difficult it is to make up for this deprivation by formal schooling, even when we try. And we have only begun to try, after accepting all too long the notion that schools should acquiesce in, even reinforce, inequalities in home backgrounds rather than overcome them.

Upgrading the earning capacity of Negroes will be difficult, but the economic effects are easy to analyze. Economists have long held that the way to reduce disparities in earned incomes is to eliminate disparities in earning capacities. If college-trained people earn more money than those who left school after eight years, the remedy is to send a larger proportion of young people to college. If machine operators earn more than ditchdiggers, the remedy is to give more people the capacity and opportunity to be machine operators. These changes in relative supplies reduce the disparity both by competing down the pay in the favored line of work and by raising the pay in the less remunerative line. When there are only a few people left in the population whose capacities are confined to garbage-collecting, it will be a high-paid calling. The same is true of domestic service and all kinds of menial work.

This classical economic strategy will be hampered if discrimination, union barriers, and the like stand in the way. It will not help to increase the supply of Negro plumbers if the local unions and contractors will not let them join. But experience also shows that barriers give way more easily when the pressures of unsatisfied demand and supply pile up.

It should therefore be the task of educational and manpower policy to engineer over the next two decades a massive change in the relative supplies of people of different educational and professional attainments and degrees of skill and training. It must be a more rapid change than has occurred in the past two decades, because that has not been fast enough to alter income differentials. We should try particularly to increase supplies in those fields where salaries and wages are already high and rising. In this process we should be very skeptical of self-serving arguments and calculations—that an increase in supply in this or that profession would be bound to reduce quality, or that there are some mechanical relations of "need" to population or to Gross National Product that cannot be exceeded.

Such a policy would be appropriate to the "war on poverty" even if there were no racial problem. Indeed, our objective is to raise the earning capacities of low-income whites as well as of Negroes. But Negroes have the most to gain, and even those who because of age or irreversible environmental handicaps must inevitably be left behind will benefit by reduction in the number of whites and other Negroes who are competing with them.

ASSURING LIVING STANDARDS IN THE
ABSENCE OF EARNING CAPACITY

The reduction of inequality in earning capacity is the fundamental solution, and in a sense anything else is stopgap. Some stopgaps are useless and even counterproductive. People who lack the capacity to earn a decent living need to be helped, but they will not be helped by minimum wage laws, trade union wage pressures, or other devices which seek to compel employers to pay them more than their work is worth. The more likely outcome of such regulations is that the intended beneficiaries are not employed at all.

A far better approach is to supplement earnings from the public fisc. But assistance can and should be given in a way that does not force the recipients out of the labor force or give them incentive to withdraw. Our present system of welfare payments does just that, causing needless waste and demoralization. This application of the means test is bad economics as well as bad sociology. It is almost as if our present programs of public assistance had been consciously contrived to perpetuate the conditions they are supposed to alleviate.

These programs apply a strict means test. The amount of assistance is an estimate of minimal needs, less the resources of the family from earnings. The purpose of the means test seems innocuous enough. It is to avoid wasting taxpayers' money on people who do not really need help. But another way to describe the means test is to note that it taxes earnings at a rate of 100 percent. A person on public assistance cannot add to his family's standard of living by working. Of course, the means test provides a certain incentive to work in order to get off public assistance altogether. But in many cases, especially where there is only one adult to provide for and take care of several children, the adult simply does not have enough time and earning opportunities to get by without financial help. He, or more likely she, is essentially forced to be both idle and on a dole. The means test also involves limitations on property holdings which deprive anyone who is or expects to be on public assistance of incentive to save.

In a society which prizes incentives for work and thrift, these are surprising regulations. They deny the country useful productive services, but that economic loss is minor in the present context. They deprive individuals and families both of work experience which could teach them skills, habits, and self-discipline of future value and of the self-respect and satisfaction which comes from improving their own lot by their own efforts.

Public assistance encourages the disintegration of the family, the key to so many of the economic and social problems of the American Negro. The main assistance program, Aid for Dependent Children, is not available if there is an able-bodied employed male in the house. In most states it is not available if there is an able-bodied man in the house, even if he is not working. All too often it is necessary for the father to leave his children so that they can eat. It is bad enough to provide incentives for idleness but even worse to legislate incentives for desertion.

The bureaucratic surveillance and guidance to which recipients of public assistance are subject undermine both their self-respect and their capacity to manage their own affairs. In the administration of assistance there is much concern to detect "cheating" against the means tests and to ensure approved prudent use of the public's money. Case loads are frequently too great and administrative regulations too confining to permit the talents of social workers to treat the roots rather than the symptoms of the social maladies of their clients. The time of the clients is considered a free good, and much of it must be spent in seeking or awaiting the attention of the officials on whom their livelihood depends.

The defects of present categorical assistance programs could be, in my opinion, greatly reduced by adopting a system of basic income allowances, integrated with and administered in conjunction with the federal income tax. In a sense the proposal is to make the income tax symmetrical. At present the federal government takes a share of family income in excess of a certain amount (for example, a married couple with three children pays no tax unless their income exceeds $3,700). The proposal is that the Treasury pay any family who falls below a certain income a fraction of the shortfall. The idea has sometimes been called a negative income tax.

The payment would be a matter of right, like an income tax refund. Individuals expecting to be entitled to payments from the government during the year could receive them in periodic installments by making a declaration of expected income and expected tax withholdings. But there would be a final settlement between the individual and the government based on a "tax" return after the year was over, just as there is now for taxpayers on April 15.

A family with no other income at all would receive a basic allowance scaled to the number of persons in the family. For a concrete example, take the basic allowance to be $400 per year per person. It might be desirable and equitable, however, to reduce the additional basic allowance for children after, say, the fourth. Once sufficient effort is being made to disseminate birth control knowledge and technique, the scale of allowances by family size certainly should provide some disincentive to the creation of large families.

A family's allowance would be reduced by a certain fraction of every dollar of other income it received. For a concrete example, take this fraction to be one-third. This means that the family has considerable incentive to earn income, because its total income including allowances will be increased by two-thirds of whatever it earns. In contrast, the means test connected with present public assistance is a 100 percent "tax" on earnings. With a one-third "tax" a family will be on the receiving end of the allowance and income tax system until its regular income equals three times its basic allowance.

Families above this "break-even" point would be taxpayers. But the less well-off among them would pay less taxes than they do now. The first dollars of income in excess of this break-even point would be taxed at the same rate as below, one-third in the example. At some income level, the tax liability so computed would be the same as the tax under the present income tax law. From that point up, the present law would take over; taxpayers with incomes above this point would not be affected by the plan.

The best way to summarize the proposal is to give a concrete graphical illustration. On the horizontal axis of Figure 1 is measured family income from wages and salaries, interest, dividends, rents, and so forth—"adjusted gross income" for the Internal Revenue Service. On the vertical axis is measured the corresponding "disposable income," that is, income after federal taxes and allowances. If the family neither paid taxes nor received allowance, disposable income would be equal to family income; in the diagram this equality would be shown by the 45° line from the origin. Disposable income above this 45° line means the family receives allowances; disposable income below this line means the family pays taxes. The broken line OAB describes the present income tax law for a married couple with three children, allowing the standard deductions. The line CD is the revision which the proposed allowance system would make for incomes below $7,963. For incomes above $7,963, the old tax schedule applies.

Beneficiaries under Federal Old Age Survivors and Disability Insurance would not be eligible for the new allowances. Congress should make sure that minimum benefits under OASDI are at least as high as the allowances. Some government payments, especially those for categorical public assistance, would eventually be replaced by basic allowances. Others, like unemployment insurance and veterans' pensions, are intended to be rights earned by past services regardless of current need. It would therefore be wrong to withhold allowances from the beneficiaries of these payments, but it would be reasonable to count them as income in determining the size of allowances, even though they are not subject to tax.

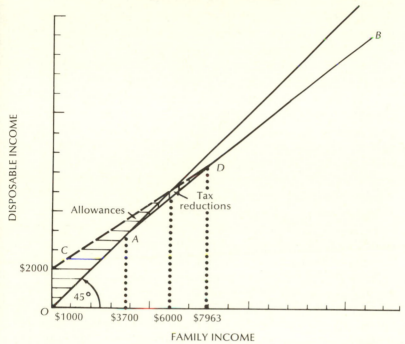

FIG. 1. *Illustration of Proposed Income Allowance Plan (married couple with three children)*

Although the numbers used above are illustrative, they are indicative of what is needed for an effective program. It would be expensive for the federal budget, involving an expenditure of perhaps $15 billion a year. Partially offsetting this budgetary cost are the savings in public assistance, on which governments now spend $5.6 billion a year, of which $3.2 billion are federal funds. In addition, savings are possible in a host of other income maintenance programs, notably in agriculture.

The program is expensive, but it need not be introduced all at once. The size of allowances can be gradually increased as room in the budget becomes available. This is likely to happen fairly rapidly. First of all, there is room right now. The budget, and the budget deficit, can and should be larger in order to create a tight labor market. Second, the normal growth of the economy increases federal revenues from existing tax rates. This is a drag on the economy, threatening stagnation and rising unemployment unless it is matched by a similar rise in federal spending or avoided by cutting taxes. With defense spending stable or declining, there is room both for increases in civilian spending, as in the war on poverty, and for further tax cuts. Gradually building an allowance system into the federal income tax would be the best way to lower the net yield of the tax—fairer and more far-reaching than further cuts in tax rates.

I referred to programs which make up for lack of earning capacity as stopgaps, but that is not entirely fair. Poverty itself saps earning capacity. The welfare way of life, on the edge of subsistence, does not provide motivation or useful work experience either to parents or to children. A better system, one which enables people to retain their self-respect and initiative, would in itself help to break the vicious circle.

The proposed allowance system is of course not the only thing which needs to be done. Without attempting to be exhaustive, I shall mention three other measures for the assistance of families without adequate earning capacity.

It hardly needs emphasizing that the large size of Negro families or nonfamilies is one of the principal causes of Negro poverty. There are too many mouths to feed per breadwinner, and frequently the care of children keeps the mother, the only possible breadwinner, at home. A program of day care and preschool education for children five and under could meet several objectives at once—enriching the experience of the children and freeing the mother for training or for work.

The quality of the medical care of Negroes is a disgrace in itself and contributes to their other economic handicaps. Even so the financing of the care of "the medically indigent" is inadequate and chaotic. Sooner or later we will extend the principle of Medicare to citizens under sixty-five. Why not sooner?

As mentioned above, much Negro poverty in the South reflects the inability of Negroes to make a livelihood in agriculture. As far as the traditional cash crop, cotton, is concerned, mechanization and the competition of larger-scale units in the Southwest are undermining the plantation and share-cropping system of the Southeast. The Negro subsistence farmer has too little land, equipment, and know-how to make a decent income. Current government agricultural programs, expensive as they are to the taxpayer, do very little to help the sharecropper or subsistence farmer. Our whole agricultural policy needs to be recast, to give income support to people rather than price support to crops and to take people off the land rather than to take land out of cultivation. The effects on the social system of the South may be revolutionary, but they can only be salutary. Obviously there will be a tremendous burden on educational and training facilities to fit people for urban and industrial life. And I must emphasize again that substantial migration from agriculture is only possible, without disaster in the cities, in a booming economy with a tight labor market.

CONCLUSION

By far the most powerful factor determining the economic status of Negroes is the overall state of the U.S. economy. A vigorously expanding economy with a steadily tight labor market will rapidly raise the position of the Negro, both absolutely and relatively. Favored by such a climate, the host of specific measures to eliminate discrimination, improve education and training, provide housing, and strengthen the family can yield substantial additional results. In a less beneficent economic climate, where jobs are short rather than men, the wars against racial inequality and poverty will be uphill battles, and some highly touted weapons may turn out to be dangerously futile.

The forces of the market place, the incentives of private self-interest, the pressures of supply and demand—these can be powerful allies or stubborn opponents. Properly harnessed, they quietly and impersonally accomplish objectives which may elude detailed legislation and administration. To harness them to the cause of the American Negro is entirely possible. It requires simply that the federal government dedicate its fiscal and monetary policies more wholeheartedly and singlemindedly to achieving and maintaining genuinely full employment. The obstacles are not technical or economic. One obstacle is a general lack of understanding that unemployment and related evils are remediable by national fiscal and monetary measures. The other is the high priority now given to competing financial objectives.

In this area, as in others, the administration has disarmed its conservative opposition by meeting it halfway, and no influential political voices challenge the tacit compromise from the "Left." Negro rights movements have so far taken no interest in national fiscal and monetary policy. No doubt gold, the federal budget, and the actions of the Federal Reserve System seem remote from the day-to-day firing line of the movements. Direct local actions to redress specific grievances and to battle visible enemies are absorbing and dramatic. They have concrete observable results. But the use of national political influence on behalf of the goals of the Employment Act of 1946 is equally important. It would fill a political vacuum, and its potential long-run payoff is very high.

The goal of racial equality suggests that the federal government should provide more stimulus to the economy. Fortunately, it also suggests constructive ways to give the stimulus. We can kill two birds with one stone. The economy needs additional spending in general; the wars on poverty and racial inequality need additional spending of particular kinds. The needed spending falls into two categories: government programs to diminish economic inequalities by building up the earning capacities of the poor and their children, and humane public assistance to citizens who temporarily or permanently lack the capacity to earn a decent living for themselves and their families. In both categories the nation, its conscience aroused by the plight of the Negro, has the chance to make reforms which will benefit the whole society.

An Economic and Social Profile
of the Negro American

RASHI FEIN

Rashi Fein, a professor of economics at the Harvard University Medical School, provides a striking portrayal of black Americans.

IN THE author's preface to *An American Dilemma*,[1] Gunnar Myrdal wrote that he was a "stranger" to the American scene and that "Things look different, depending upon 'where you stand.'" It is also true that things look different, depending upon where you look. The profile of the Negro American is a changing profile. What one sees depends on what one looks at, on the period that one examines, and on the comparisons one makes. Our profile will not "look." It will "look different" or "look similar." Without comparisons its significance would be limited. . . .

The frame of reference, the relevant comparison in drawing an economic and social profile and in understanding the significance of the data that make up the profile, is a comparison between the Negro and other Americans. Such comparisons are given increased dimension when the data examined represent the positions of the two groups at different moments in time. For if we are to understand the attitudes, aspirations, and accomplishments of the Negro American, we need to know not only where he is, but also how he got there, how rapidly conditions have been changing, what has been happening to his relative position. Others may consider whether the most significant influence on the psychology and attitudes of the Negro is where he stands in relation to the white, where he stands in relation to his parents and grandparents, how his status relative to whites compares with the relative status of his parents and grandparents in an earlier period, or a mixture of these that takes account of relative progress as well as relative position. Surely, however, all have some measure of influence.

The frame of reference developed in this essay differs from

those most frequently used in analyzing the Negro's progress. It is generally customary either: (1) to compare Negro attainment today with the level of Negro attainment at some earlier time (for example, the Negro maternal mortality rate in 1960 was 98 per 100,000 live births, down from 774 in 1940) or (2) to compare Negro-white differentials today with Negro-white differentials in some earlier period (for example, in 1960 the Negro maternal mortality rate was 3.8 times the white rate while in 1955 it had been 4.0 times). In general, the first type of comparison shows significant improvement—Negroes (just as is true for whites) *are* better off than their grandparents were. But how one assesses one's own situation is, and should be, influenced by how others are faring at the same time. It is true that the second comparison does take account of Negro progress relative to white progress and does attempt to measure where the Negro finds himself in relation to other Americans. It is thus more meaningful than the first comparison. Nevertheless, it is often difficult to interpret. Because white-nonwhite differentials are large and because the rates of change of white and nonwhite indices are different, we sometimes find that the absolute differences between white and nonwhite indicators behave differently than do the ratios of the same indicators. In 1940, for example, the absolute difference between the white and nonwhite infant mortality rate was 31 per 1,000 live births, while in 1962 the difference had declined to 19 per 1,000. Yet in 1940 nonwhite infant mortality was 70 percent greater than that of whites and in 1962 it was 90 percent greater. . . . Sometimes, too, differentials are narrowed because nonwhite indicators are improving (slowly, but improving) while white indicators—perhaps pressing against limits of present knowledge—have reached a plateau. The important consideration, however, is that the narrowing differential fails to take account of a frequent and significant phenomenon: the nonwhite is moving up more slowly than the white did when, many years ago, the white stood where the nonwhite now is. That comparison—between speed of movement over the same range of experience—is relevant in assessing recent developments and the possibilities for the future.

The measure I introduce is simple yet informative. Where data permit, I calculate a time-lag statistic: how many years earlier did the white American—with the full range of opportunity open to him—attain the particular level (say, of health, education, income) that the Negro—so long denied that opportunity—has reached only today. I ask also whether this gap (in years) is greater or less than at earlier times (that is, was the Negro more years behind in some earlier period). I thus compare the relative speed of movement over the same range of experience. The change in the length of the gap depends upon the relative rates of change of white and Negro indicators over time. The results are disturbing: in a number of cases the time gap has been widening rather than narrowing. Today the Negro is further behind the white (in years) than he once was.

An illustration may be helpful. Table 1 presents hypothetical data on level of health attainment: the higher the index, the better the health level.

TABLE 1. *Hypothetical Health Levels, White and Negro, Selected Years*

	1900	1920	1940	1960
1. White	100	200	250	275
2. Negro	—	100	150	200
3. Absolute differential (1–2)	—	100	100	75
4. White-Negro ratio (1 ÷ 2)	—	2	1.67	1.375
5. Time gap (years by which Negro progress lags white)	—	20	30	40

The data show a narrowing of differentials in the period 1920–1960 (from 100 down to 75; from a factor of 2 down to 1.375). Yet, whereas the Negro in 1920 was where the white of 1900 had been, that gap of twenty years had widened to forty years by 1960 (in 1960 the Negro was where the white had been in 1920). This occurred because the white had moved from 100 to 200 in two decades, but conditions prevented the Negro from doing so well: in this hypothetical example it takes Negroes four (not two) decades to cover the same terrain. This comparison, the reader will note, focuses on movement over the same range of experience (100 to 200) rather than on movement over the same time period (1920 to 1960). This is its strength, for it helps center attention on the process of growth and on prospects for the near future. In this example it suggests that special efforts will be required if previous growth rates are to be sharply boosted and the time gap narrowed. For if the Negro does only as well as the white once did in moving from an index of 200 to 275, it will take the Negro forty years to achieve equality—even if the white were to make no more progress.

Let me make clear that I do not imply that all groups should be expected to follow the same growth path. Each group—ethnic, racial, religious—in American life has its unique characteristics and is the product of its unique experiences. The "baggage" the Negro brings with him—the traditions, the strengths, the handicaps—is different from that brought by others. Furthermore, the gap (in years) may widen or narrow due to erratic behavior of white indices—unrelated to discrimination against Negroes. Such patterns must be examined carefully. But often the difference in speed of upward movement between Negro and white Americans is—in a broad way—an indication of the effects of present and past differences in opportunity. It is cause for concern.

It is important to recognize that if the Negro in 1965 is where the white was in 1945, this does not mean that the Negro considers himself as well off as the white considered himself twenty years ago. Nor should he. The Negro today is aware that a very substantial majority of the nation has higher income, more education, better health, and so forth than he does. The Negro stands below the median indices for the nation. But this was not true of the white twenty years ago. He did not suffer the psychological disadvantage of being behind—for he was not behind. He was the median American. Thus the situation is vastly different for the Negro who has an income of $3,000 when most other Americans have more, than it was for the white when he had $3,000 in income and that was the average for the nation. In a psychological sense—and this molds attitudes toward the problem—the Negro is even further behind than the data show.

The comparison of white-nonwhite differentials is not meant to suggest that every index should be the same for each and every group (or person). America is a land of many tongues and tastes. Different cultures and value systems will reflect themselves in different behabior patterns and thus in socioeconomic indicators. But the indicators selected measure aspects that surely all groups feel are of importance. We all desire lower infant mortality rates, lower unemployment rates, and so forth. Differentials in the particular indicators selected, therefore, tend to reflect differences in equality of opportunity rather than deliberate choices.

In some future year we will surely reach a stage where it will be difficult to judge the significance of differences in white-non-white indices (unless we foolishly define white indices as always the desirable standard and incorrectly assume that white middle-class values are the only "proper" values). This difficulty is clear, for example, in regard to occupational structure. Underrepresentation in some occupations can only occur in conjunction with overrepresentation in other occupations. Surely there is nothing undesirable if, as a consequence of group values and traditions, individuals *choose* to enter a particular occupation, thus resulting in group "overrepresentation" in that occupation and "underrepresentation" in some other. Today, however, it is unhappily all too clear that Negro underrepresentation in the professions, for example, is not the result of a desire to move into unskilled labor. The point at issue is that we look forward not to a situation where everyone is identical and the nonwhite is 10 percent of every occupation, geographic region, and so forth—but to a situation where he could be that (or more) in any given sector if he so desired. . . .

We begin at birth. The child is born. In 1959–61 the Negro male had a life expectancy of 61.5 years at birth. His white counterpart first reached that level in 1931–33, twenty-eight years earlier (and has not dipped below it since 1937–39). In 1959–61 the white male life expectancy at birth was 67.6 years, 6 years more than the nonwhite. But the point is not that Negro life expectancy in years is 91 percent of white, but that the Negro male child today is where the white was some twenty-two to twenty-eight years earlier. This is the gap of which we speak.

We know more than that. Already in 1921–23 the white had reached a life expectancy level the Negro was not to attain until 1949–51 (thus in 1950 the gap also was twenty-eight years). In 1940 the gap had been twenty-seven years. We have not been making progress in cutting the time gap. It is often easy to forget that the speed of progress is in part dependent on where one starts. . . . In 1900 white male life expectancy at birth was 48.2 years—by 1940, it was 62.8 years—a gain of 15 years in four decades. But for the Negro, too, a full forty years were needed to progress over the same range: from 47.1 years in 1920 to 61.5 years in 1960. . . . The fact that one group made greater progress *over the same chronological time period* than did another may result from the fact that it was in a different range of its (nonlinear) growth curve. If, however, rates of progress are compared over a range common to both groups, we may find —and in this example we do find—that Negro progress was no more rapid than was earlier white progress. . . .

The significance of the measure should be clear. The Negro covered the same territory from 1920 to 1960 that the white had covered from 1900 to 1940—the same territory in the same length of time. But we would have expected that, given equal opportunity, he would have moved more rapidly. It should be easier for 10 percent of the population to advance more rapidly (if the other 90 percent care) than for 90 percent to advance. Furthermore, the state of scientific knowledge was greater in 1920 than in 1900, greater in 1930 than in 1910, and so on, thus permitting a compression of the time required to make an equal amount of progress. . . . It is here contended that were the Negro to have made his advance only as rapidly as had the white there would be cause for concern (and action). But he was prevented from doing even that well. The often-cited advantages of being late did not accrue to the Negro. The time gap has not been materially shortened in the last four decades. . . .

In 1960 the chances that the Negro infant would die before reaching its first birthday were 43 per 1,000 live births—double that of a white baby. This rate was achieved by whites two decades earlier, in 1940. The gap is twenty years. In 1950 the Negro had been where the white was only about eleven years earlier (the gap had been seventeen years in 1940 and fifteen years in 1930). Thus, while the infant mortality rate for whites dropped from 100 per 1,000 to 43 per 1,000 in twenty-five years, it took the Negro thirty years to cover the same distance. Progress, as indicated by narrowing and widening of the gap, was uneven. In some decades progress was more rapid, in other decades less rapid. In the decade of the 1930s Negroes covered a range that whites covered in eight years (1915–1923); in the 1940s Negroes covered a range that had taken whites fifteen years, but in the entire decade of the 1950s Negroes made no more progress than whites had made in a tenth of a decade—in one year.

This is the case because infant mortality for the total population (chiefly white) decreased by about 4.3 percent each year from 1933 to 1949 and by 2.0 percent from 1950 to 1960. For nonwhites the rate decreased by 4.6 percent from 1933 to 1949 but only by 1.2 percent from 1950 to 1956 and in 1960 the rate was what it had been in 1956. Thus in 1960 the rate of nonwhite infant mortality was 1.9 times that of white in 1960, while in 1950 it had been 1.7 times as high. . . .

The Negro child faces a different world than does today's white baby. So does his family. The mortality rate for his older brother, age twenty, is somewhat over twenty years behind the white mortality rate; the gap for his father is perhaps forty years and for his grandfather exceeds sixty years. . . .

Thus the Negro male child is born into a world in which (in 1962) his chances of reaching age twenty are about the same as that of a white's reaching thirty-seven. A Negro girl (at birth) has the same chances of attaining age twenty as a white girl has of reaching forty-two. The lags are almost two decades.

We turn to education. The educational attainment of nonwhite adults with whom the child comes in contact is greater than was the attainment of adults whom the 1940 child met. Our child's parents have more education than their parents had. In 1960 the median school years completed by nonwhites twenty-five years old and over was 8.2 years. In 1940 the median number completed by nonwhites then twenty-five years and older was only 5.8 years. Yet already in 1940 white attainment was 8.7 years, a level higher than Negro attainment twenty years later. The gap, therefore, exceeds twenty years. It can be noted, too, that the white median rose from 8.7 in 1940 to 10.9 in 1960 (a rise of 2.2 years) while nonwhite attainment—in spite of the start from a lower base—rose by only 2.4 years (5.8–8.2). The difference, though not great, does represent a reversal of the 1920–1940 experience. Much of the rise in the nonwhite median is explained by the substantial drop in the percentage of Negroes with very little education (in 1940, 71 percent of persons twenty-five years old and over had completed less than eight years of schooling, but by 1960 this was reduced to 47 percent; in 1920, 45 percent of those aged twenty-five to twenty-nine had less than five years of school; by 1940 this was true of only 27 percent of those aged twenty-five to twenty-nine, and by 1960 it was true of only 7 percent). Nevertheless, the absolute increase in the percentage of whites completing high school or college was greater than was the increase for nonwhites. In 1960 the percentage of Negroes twenty-five years old and over who had completed college (3.5 percent) was substantially less than the percentage had been for whites in 1940 (4.9 percent). Even in 1960 the percentage of Negro male college graduates aged twenty-five to twenty-nine (5.3 percent) was only equal to the percentage among whites in 1920 and the percentage of high-school graduates in that age group was about the same as among whites in 1940.[2]

Educational attainment is related to future employment possibilities. The demand for educated personnel has increased. It can, therefore, be seen that in a very real sense nonwhites without a college education in 1960 were at a competitive disadvantage vis-à-vis the rest of the labor force as compared with the competitive disadvantage in 1920 for whites with the same educational attainment. Nonwhites with less than a high-school degree in 1960 were similarly at a disadvantage as compared with white nonhigh-school graduates in 1940. The educational gap—as it would influence employment possibilities—is even greater and more significant than suggested.

Nevertheless, I cannot subscribe to the view that the Negro faces insurmountable problems in entering the world of work. It is said that technological progress is so much more rapid today than in earlier periods—a statement that itself is probably incorrect—that the Negro is falling further and further behind the educational requirements imposed by modern industry. Some conclude, therefore, that earlier minority groups had a considerable advantage over today's Negro. Were there no discrimination in employment, it is doubtful that this would be the case. It is true that educational requirements advance even as the Negro American's educational level advances. Some of the gains that would lead to upgrading are, therefore, "dissipated." But not all the gains are wasted. The rise in educational attainment of younger Negroes, in particular, is very rapid, and the absolute attainment (outside the South) quite high. Earlier minority groups faced a less demanding economy, but also had less educational attainment to offer. It is not clear that on balance, *and abstracting from discrimination,* the situation is significantly *more* disadvantageous to the Negro. . . .

While data to compare educational attainment as far back through time as we would like are unavailable, a tracing through time can be approximated by comparing persons in various age groups today. In 1964, 16 percent of Negro males aged twenty to twenty-four had one or more years of college—the same percentage as among white males aged fifty-five to sixty-four, most of whom received their college education thirty-five to forty years ago. Thus, in terms of the percentage with some college education, the young Negro of today is barely attaining what whites who today are fifty-five to sixty-four years old attained when they were young. This represents a gap of over thirty-five years. The gap, though still considerable, is much shorter at lower levels of educational attainment.

Nor is the educational gap between generations always narrowing. As the Bureau of the Census reports, "It thus appears that not only is the nonwhite population more poorly educated than the white population but the net gain of nonwhites at higher levels of education, as calculated from educational differences in the fathers' and sons' generations, has not been as great as for whites." The gap is a generation: in 1962, 10.3 percent of the fathers of white males aged twenty to sixty-four had some college education (and 25.6 percent of the sons did) while 10.4 percent of Negro males aged twenty to sixty-four (the "sons") had some college (and 4.4 percent of the fathers did). Thus the percentage among white fathers was the same as among Negro sons. . . .

Unfortunately it is impossible to develop an adequate time-lag measure for a number of relevant indices—and certainly impossible to compare the length of lag back through time. The reason is clear. Even today the Negro-white differential is so great and adequate statistics are of such recent vintage that the white was already ahead of today's nonwhite attainment when data were first gathered (or shortly thereafter). In such cases more traditional methods must be used to make comparisons over time. Sometimes these difficulties are compounded by the fact that the data are subject to significant cyclical variation (as is the case, for example, with unemployment rates). If, in those cases, earlier years are cited in which the index for whites equaled today's Negro index, this is not done in order to suggest a time-lag measure. Rather, referring to specific earlier years may help remind the (white) reader of what things were like then. Thus, if one wants to understand what an unemployment rate of 20 percent represents, it is helpful to be reminded that this was the national rate in 1935.

Let us examine unemployment. Today the Negro faces an unemployment situation unknown to the white for almost two and one-half decades—and the Negro has been facing it for a number of years. What is recession for the white (say, an unemployment rate of 6 percent) is prosperity for the nonwhite. In 1964, when the total unemployment rate for white males twenty years old and over was 3.4 percent, the nonwhite rate was over twice as high—7.7 percent. The rate for Negro females aged twenty and over was almost twice as high as for whites, and this was also the case for males and females combined (aged fourteen to nineteen). In 1964—a prosperity year—the Negro confronted an unemployment rate (9.8 percent) more than 50 percent higher than the highest rate faced by whites at any time since the great depression. Surely, the Negro must feel wry as he considers the debate about the level of unemployment that shall be considered full employment. His employment rate has reached the "interim target" of 4.0 percent only twice in the postwar period.

Let me make it clear that I do not say that the Negro fails to share in upward movements of the economy. He does share in prosperity—just as he is hurt by recessions. There *are* differences between unemployment rates for Negro males of 4.4 percent in 1953, 13.7 percent in 1958, and 9.1 percent in 1964. It is a fact, however, that Negro unemployment rates are higher than white rates at the same moment in time and that the Negro *frequently* faces unemployment rates which—if faced by all workers—would be considered a national scandal. The fact is that the unemployment rate for Negroes in 1964, a year of general prosperity, was over one and one-half times as large as that for whites in *any* of the postwar recessions. Therefore, perhaps, it is appropriate to say that whites fluctuate between prosperity and recession but Negroes fluctuate between depression and great depression.

The difference in overall white and Negro unemployment rates is not explained entirely by a different age-sex structure. Negro unemployment rates for every age-sex grouping (except for women over fifty-five) are higher—sometimes far higher—than the highest postwar rate for whites in the same age-sex group. We spoke of *fluctuations* between depression and great or deep depression. But for some of the age-sex groups—particularly, but not exclusively, among teenagers—unemployment rates appear perpetually high: the unemployment rate for male Negroes aged sixteen and seventeen was last below 20 percent in 1957 (it reached 31 percent in 1961); it was last below 19 percent for males aged eighteen and nineteen in 1956.

The differential in unemployment rates presents a real and severe problem. It is a problem requiring special attention and strong specific (as well as general) measures. Indeed, it may require relatively stronger action than would have been necessary fifteen years ago. . . .

And when the Negro is unemployed, it is for a longer period of time. In 1964, nonwhites represented 11 percent of the labor force and 21 percent of the unemployed, but they accounted for 23 percent of those unemployed fifteen weeks or longer and 25 percent of those unemployed for over half a year. In 1963, 27 percent of white, but 35 percent of nonwhite unemployed males were unemployed fifteen weeks or more and 14 percent of white but 20 percent of nonwhite unemployed males were unemployed twenty-seven weeks or more. The average duration of unemployment for white males was slightly under fifteen weeks, for non-whites slightly over nineteen.

Finally, it should be noted that Negroes, when employed, are more likely to be working only part time. In 1963, for example, while 81 percent of whites at work in nonagricultural industries worked full time, this was true of only 74 percent of nonwhites. Only 3.1 percent of whites worked part time for economic reasons —slack work, inability to find full-time work—but this was the case for 9.6 percent of employed nonwhites. The average number of hours worked by those employed was 8 percent higher for white males than for nonwhite males.

The Negro faces higher unemployment rates, more frequent periods of unemployment in a given year, longer duration of unemployment, more part-time rather than full-time work—and all this is true even when occupation is held constant. The often-heard comment that the differentials result from the fact that nonwhites have a disadvantageous occupational structure is only partly true. . . .

Thus our Negro child grows up in a world in which opportunity seems closed. And surely his aspirations are in part influenced by the achievements of other Negroes. In 1960, when 10 percent of the male experienced labor force was nonwhite, only 3.5 percent of male professionals, technical, and kindred workers were nonwhite (and perhaps one-quarter of these were not Negro). Only 1.4 percent of accountants and auditors were nonwhite, 1.7 percent of engineers, 1.3 percent of lawyers and judges, 1.3 percent of salaried managers, officials, and proprietors, 2.0 percent of bookkeepers (and 6.8 percent of clerical and kindred workers), 2.1 percent of sales workers, and 4.9 percent of craftsmen, foremen, and kindred workers (all data for males only). But the 10 percent proportion of the labor force was exceeded in some occupations: 48.4 percent of private household workers are nonwhite, 26.1 percent of laborers, and we find large percentages for other occupations at the bottom rungs of the occupational ladder. . . .

The difference in educational attainment accounts for much, but not all, of the difference found in occupational structure. In 1962, for example, 20 percent of nonwhite male high-school graduates were laborers. This was true of only 4 percent of white male high-school graduates. Even among white males with an elementary education or less, the equivalent percentage was only 9 percent. Nineteen percent of nonwhite females with some college were private household workers but this was virtually unknown (1 percent) among white females who had attended college. It was not even as high as 19 percent (only 13 percent) for white females with zero to eight years of elementary school.

The interrelation of the various parts of our description is depressing—the relative disadvantage in one area causes and is caused by disadvantages in another area. Relatively high unemployment and a disadvantageous occupational structure, for example, both contribute to lower incomes for Negroes than for whites. We now examine income patterns. What are our Negro child's chances in that area?

In 1964 the Negro family with income had a median income of $3,839—only 56 percent of that for white families. White families had reached a $3,800 income level back in 1951, but the situation is worse than is implied by his thirteen-year gap. Negroes in 1964 purchased commodities at 1964 prices, while whites in 1951 purchased at substantially lower 1951 prices. If we correct for price changes and compare income in dollars with 1964 purchasing power, we find that white income, even as far back as 1947, exceeded present Negro income by, perhaps, 10 to 15 percent. Census data permit more detailed analysis. Using constant 1959 dollars (dollars with the same purchasing power), we find that in 1960 13.7 percent of all Negro families had annual total money income of under $1,000 and 32.1 percent had incomes of under $2,000. Even as long ago as 1947 this was true of only 6.5 percent and 19.1 percent of all white families. The lag is found among urban, rural nonfarm, and rural farm families (Table 2).

TABLE 2. *Median Annual Money Income and Percentage of Families Below Specified Income Levels by Residence and Color, 1947 and 1960*

(Income levels expressed in dollars with 1959 purchasing power)

	Median income	Percent of Families Below $1,000	Below $2,000
Urban nonwhite 1960	$3,844	7.0	21.8
Urban white 1947	4,544	3.6	10.8
Rural nonfarm nonwhite 1960	2,000	24.8	50.0
Rural nonfarm white 1947	3,809	6.6	17.0
Rural farm nonwhite 1960	1,155	44.0	77.3
Rural farm white 1947	2,827	16.4	34.9

In 1960 the urban nonwhite caught up to the 1947 level for rural nonfarm whites. The urban white had, of course, achieved this level many years before 1947. To say that in 1960 the *urban* Negro family had the same real money income that the white *rural nonfarm* family had in 1947, to say that in 1960 the median Negro family had an income equal to the median white *farm* family is to point up the substantial lag and gap in income. . . .

If we use a poverty standard—families with incomes under $3,000—the chances in 1963 were 43 in 100 that our child was born into a family in poverty (by 1964 the chances were down to 37 in 100). It is of course true, as many have pointed out, that the large majority of poor families are white (after all, an even greater majority of all families are white). A program to eliminate poverty cannot, therefore, be successful if it addresses itself only to Negroes. However, the Negro has a far greater chance (almost three times as great) of being in poverty than does the white. Even as late as 1963 the percentage of Negro families in poverty was 50 percent higher than the white level had been sixteen years earlier in 1947 (measured in 1963 constant dollars). To whom can we ask the Negro to compare himself if he is to have some degree of hope? Apparently only to himself at some earlier period—in 1947 two-thirds of Negro families were poor—but not to the rest of America which already in 1947 was better off than the Negro was in 1963 and which, since 1947, had a decline of 30 percent in the number of poor families while the number of poor Negro families (in part as a result of the increase in the absolute number of families) *increased* by 2 percent.

In discussions of income data, the point is often, and validly, made that the worker's educational attainment is an important determinant of income. It is surely small comfort for the Negro to be told that his present low income status is due to his lack of education. Explanations do not assist in making purchases; only money does. . . . But there is a difficulty with this—even aside from the fact that the Negro's low educational attainment itself is the result of discrimination. The difficulty is that low education does not provide the total explanation for low income. As with a number of variables already discussed, simply being Negro also makes a difference. For in 1963 our Negro child's family had a median income of $4,530 if the family head completed high school. But the white family with the same years of education for the head had an income of $6,997—almost 55 percent more. Indeed, if the white had but eight years of schooling, his income was $5,454, 20 percent more than for the Negro high-school graduate. Nor are these unfavorable comparisons isolated cases: The Negro family whose head had some high school earned less than the white with fewer than eight years of schooling; *the Negro who has attended (but not completed) college earns less than the white with only eight years of elementary school,* the Negro college graduate earns but slightly more than does the white high-school graduate. Surely there are differences in the quality of education. In parts of the nation a year of Negro education was not (and is not) equal to a year of white education. Nevertheless, to argue that there is no discrimination in employment and income requires that we argue that the Negro with some college knows no more than does the white with only eight years of elementary school. This is hard to accept. . . .

It is important to realize the story these data tell. . . . It is a simple fact that the Negro is *qualified* for higher occupational levels and for higher incomes than he attains. The data document a story of discrimination. Some may pessimistically conclude that it is harder to eliminate discrimination than to raise levels of education. I would respond that, painful as is the story the data reveal, there are grounds for optimism. We need not wait until today's and tomorrow's (better educated) youths become adults to increase incomes and raise occupational levels. Discrimination may be harder to combat than poor education—though even this is not certain. But it can be combated *in the short run*. To raise education and reap its rewards must take time—considerable time. But if discrimination accounts for much (though not all) of the income disparity—and I conclude that it does—we can make more rapid, more immediate progress. Perhaps as little as one-third of the total disparity between white and nonwhite incomes is due to fewer years of education. Corrections for quality of education and geographic distribution of population would lower the proportion that can be accounted for by discrimination. Nevertheless, substantial income increases could result—even with today's educational levels—as a consequence of the elimination of discrimination. Surely we favor better and more education, but we need not wait for the effects of today's better education to take hold a decade hence. . . .

How low the family's income is will depend, in part, on the region in which the family resides. But the differences between white and nonwhite income are large in all regions. First, income is reduced because, while almost two-thirds of white families are headed by a year-round full-time worker, only one-half of Negro families are so headed. These differences are found in all regions except the West. Furthermore, family income— even if the head is fully employed—is lower for the nonwhite (again in all regions): In the Northeast it is 70 percent of white, in the North Central 83 percent, in the South 51 percent, and in the West 86 percent. If account is taken of lower full-time employment as well as lower earnings, the percentage that nonwhite family income is of white family income drops significantly to 65, 73, 45, and 76 percent respectively for the four regions. Clearly, there are large differences among regions. Equally clearly, the situation is an unhappy one in all regions.

Our Negro child has been born into a family that is substantially poorer than the average white family. In part, this is because the Negro family head has less education than the white, earns less even at the same levels of education, has less chance

TABLE 3. *Median Income and Median Years of School Completed, Total Population and Nonwhite, by Occupation, 1959*

Occupation	Median income		Median years of school completed	
	Nonwhite	Total	Nonwhite	Total
Bakers	$3354	$4633	8.9	9.2
Carpenters	2320	4271	8.1	9.3
Welders and flame-cutters	4454	5116	9.6	9.7
Elevator operators	3122	3487	8.7	8.6
Automobile mechanics	3173	4372	8.9	9.9
Tinsmiths, coppersmiths, and sheet metal workers	4710	5542	11.1	10.8

of year-round full-time employment. All this most of us know. But startling is the fact that there had been very little change in the ratio of nonwhite family income to white family income through 1965 (there had been extremely rapid progress in the first half of the decade of the 1940s). In 1947 the ratio of non-white to white family income was 0.51 and, though it reached 0.57 in 1952 (with progress from 1950 to 1952), it had fallen back to 0.51 in 1958 and stood at 0.56 in 1964. There has been some progress since 1964, however, as the income ratio increased to 0.62 in 1972. Progress in reducing the disparity in income ratios has been concentrated in periods of tight labor markets (parts of the 1940s, 1950s, and late 1960s), but it is unfortunate for all of us and most unfortunate for Negroes that many years have passed since the United States has faced tight labor markets.

What does lower Negro income mean for the living conditions in which our child is raised? We turn to the family's housing. The quality of housing occupied by Negroes is—as we know—markedly inferior to that occupied by whites. Since 1920, when the number of persons per occupied dwelling unit was the same for whites and nonwhites, the rate for whites has declined from 4.3 persons to 3.3 persons per unit in 1960, while the figure for nonwhites has declined only from 4.3 to 4.0. More significant, however, are the figures on the number of persons per room—a crowding measure. In 1960, 14 percent of nonwhite units had over 1.5 persons per room (down from 23 percent in 1940), and 28 percent had more than 1 person per room (down from 40 percent in 1940). But comparable 1960 figures for white units were only 2 percent with more than 1.5 persons per room and 10 percent with more than 1 person per room. Already in 1940 the white child was doing his homework under less crowded conditions than our Negro child faced twenty years later. . . .

Thus overcrowding is not uncommon in Negro housing. But the situation is made worse by the quality of what is overcrowded. . . . In 1960 our family lived in housing that had not reached 1950 U.S. standards on hot and cold water inside the structure or on bathing facilities and had barely reached 1950 standards for toilet facilities.

The Negro thus is more likely to be living in an overcrowded unit that lacks a number of modern facilities. In addition, in 1960 the chances were six times greater (than for whites) that the structure he lived in was dilapidated and two and one-half times greater that it was deteriorating. . . .

The child with whom we began our story thus has shorter life expectancy, lives in less desirable housing, is a member of a family with less education, with a less favorable occupational structure, with more unemployment, and with lower income than the median white baby born at the same time. And the rate of improvement in these indices still leaves the Negro far behind the average for the rest of America.

But, of course, there is no *the* Negro American—as there is no *the* white American. There are many Negro Americans who live in conditions far better than the median Negro American. There are some who live better than the median American [regardless of color]. There are many who live in far worse conditions. Geographic location makes an important difference in the indices cited. Our child has a better than even chance of being born in the South where the situation is generally even poorer than is indicated by the national data previously cited. It is a fact that the Negro in the North lives very differently than does the Negro in the South—though not so well as many whites believe or would like to believe. Table 4 illustrates some of these differences. In this table the status of Negroes in Census divisions with extreme highs and lows is shown. For purposes of comparison the median white U.S. averages are also shown.

Though there is significant variation in some of the indicators, in no case is performance in the division with greatest Negro attainment equal to the white median for the entire United States.

TABLE 4. *Range of Values for Selected Indices for Nonwhites in Census Divisions and U.S. Median for Whites* *

| | Nonwhite | | White |
	In "Poorest" Division	In "Best" Division	U.S.
Infant mortality per 1,000 live births (1962)	46.9 (ESC)	30.7 (P)	22.3
Median school years completed (1960)	6.7 (ESC)	10.3 (P)	10.9
Percent college graduates, of males 25–29 (1960)	3.6 (ESC)	9.8 (P)	15.6
Percent housing sound with all plumbing (1960)	23.1 (ESC)	70.9 (P)	79.7
Percent housing with more than one person per room (1960)	46.0 (M)	18.2 (NE)	9.8
Family income (1963)	$2520 (S)	$5417 (W)	$6548
Percent families with income under $3,000 (1963)	58.4 (S)	19.8 (W)	15.9

* "ESC" stands for the East South Central division; "P" for Pacific; "NE" for New England; "M" for Mountain; "S" for South; and "W" for West.

The significant differences between South and North and between urban and rural areas, combined with the very considerable migration of Negroes from the South to the North and from rural areas to urban areas, help explain much of the improvement over time in many of the indices we have examined. But progress in the future will require upward movement *within* the urban setting since the heaviest rural-urban migration has already taken place. In 1960, 73 percent of all Negro Americans had urban residences—a higher percentage than was true for whites. South to North migration, it is true, continues. But the situation is far from satisfactory when the national median for Negroes increases relative to whites only as a consequence of population redistribution even as relative declines occur in all regions.

The differentials that exist between the majority of whites and the majority of the Negro minority are great. The lack of opportunity and the previous (and present) discriminatory practices have had their consequences: In many respects the Negro is today living in a world the white has long since left behind. The gains the Negro has made and is making are substantial—all indicators are advancing. The real situation today is better than it once was. Nevertheless, we dare not overestimate the extent of these gains or underestimate the distance still to be covered.

Though the gains are large relative to where an earlier generation of Negroes stood, they are often more limited if the comparison is made of nonwhite indicators relative to those for whites. In such comparisons (for example, income), we often find that the differential between whites and nonwhites has been widening in recent years. Differentials frequently narrowed in the 1940s but increased again in the latter part of the 1950s. To the economist this underlines the importance of full employment and high-level economic growth in helping to secure advances. Everything is interrelated: Education has an impact on health, and employment on income, and income on education, and so forth. Advances are, therefore, required on a broad front. The generation now growing up will have opportunities opened to them—opportunities to make these advances—that their fathers did not have. But the record of the 1940s and 1950s tells us that these opportunities and the ability to seize them will be greater, the more rapid the growth and expansion of the economy.

Surely, however, the data indicate that the differentials are now so wide and the distance to be covered so great that simply waiting for time to bring improvement is to indulge in unjustified optimism. Many of the nonwhite indicators have not been advancing so rapidly as did the white indicators when they were at comparable levels. It is often taking the Negro longer to move up from "a" to "b" than it took the white. In many cases the narrowing of present differentials results from a redistribution of Negro population—and a "plateauing" of white rates of progress. But "plateauing" could also occur for nonwhites. We cannot be sanguine if we find, for example ,that in 1950 the Negro reached levels that the white achieved in 1920 (a gap of thirty years), but that by 1960 he was where the white was in 1925 (a gap of thirty-five years). This kind of advance does not give us confidence concerning the achievement of equality in the not too distant future.

But optimism *is* warranted if concern leads us to take measures directed at the problem. For at no previous time in recent history could measures be so easily taken and progress so readily result. We have the knowledge, and the means are available.

And the numbers of persons involved make the problem even easier of solution, for Negroes represent only about 10 percent of the population (with, perhaps, 5 percent of the income). The "burden" of special measures, when addressed to 10 percent but borne by the whole society, is, therefore, not great. This cost—when borne in a growing economy—can be absorbed while everyone advances.

And, it should be clear that the gains would not accrue solely to the nonwhite. The raising of Negro education, health, productivity, and employment would increase the economy's bounty for all. (The President's Council of Economic Advisers estimates that in time there would be an increase perhaps of as much as $23 billion—measured at today's price levels—in the Gross National Product.) In addition, the indirect benefits to all of advances in education, health, and such in part of the population—while difficult to measure—are significant. Finally, and most importantly, if we remember that the Negro American is not only a Negro but an American, it should be clear that his gains are our gains—gains by all America.

These conclusions do not in themselves suggest how changes in the present situation are to be brought about—how rates of change are to be accelerated. I have already alluded to a number of situations that have policy implications. I summarize them.

I note again that some argue that the external world the Negro faces is vastly different from that faced by other minority groups in the past and that timing has conspired to rob the Negro of his opportunities. He, the argument asserts, is trying to make speedy progress when automation and increased stress on skills make job entrance more difficult and job requirements more demanding. For these reasons, if for no other, the Negro is said to be at a considerable disadvantage compared to other minorities. I agree that the Negro faces a *different* world. However, relative to the Negro American's achievements and accomplishments, it is not clear that, *were there no discrimination,* it would be a harsher world. The economy does place an additional premium on persons with more training—but in 1964 the median number of school years completed by Negroes aged twenty to twenty-four was 12.0 years. This is a far higher educational level than previous generations of Negroes—or previous minority groups—possessed. True it is that technological progress will bring a shift in occupational structure—but this will help unlock opportunities that free the Negro. It is to be preferred to an economic structure that demands less skill but provides less room for upward mobility. In this, as in other areas, expansion, growth, and change are the vital ingredients in Negro advancement. For it is easier to effect advancement for the Negro in a world of change than in a world of rigidity. Free education, expansion of university enrollments, greater concern about poverty, illiteracy, public health, housing codes, economic security—all these surely mean greater opportunity for present and future generations of Negro Americans. The importance of this concern—and commitment—cannot be overemphasized. It is a source of change and of ultimate strength. It is found in many sectors of society, organized and unorganized, public and private. It need not be ephemeral. It is the task of all—perhaps, particularly of the Negro—to keep the fire of concern burning brightly.

Such concern has—and will continue to have—its impact on public and private action—on legislation, on its implementation, and on private (business and nonbusiness) behavior. The catalogue of actions is a long one; it encompasses the daily behavior of individuals and enterprises. What is required is that these actions, that the behavior, be nondiscriminatory, that equality be practiced as well as promised.

The data bear out the fact that a substantial part of America's problem results not only from past but also from present discriminatory behavior, not from objective, quantifiable "shortcomings" of the Negro—for example, less education—but from subjective attitudes of the white. "Men at some times are masters of their fates: The fault, dear Brutus, is not in our stars, But in ourselves, that we are underlings." The fault *is* in *ourselves* (not in the Negro), and we are masters of our fates. We can do much even today without waiting for the educational advancements that bear fruit tomorrow. We can eliminate present discrimination even as we institute programs that help remove the disabilities caused by past discrimination. We can reverse the "slippage" the data reveal.

Elimination of discrimination means a different sharing of the nation's (more abundant) products. I stress that a more equitable division is more easily achieved when the amount of product is growing. This is particularly true if conditions are such that the institution of nondiscriminatory programs—and of compensatory, supplemental, and upgrading programs—is advantageous to those undertaking them, that is, if it becomes disadvantageous and expensive to indulge in the "taste" for discrimination and prejudice or to maintain the status quo.

The Negro did advance more rapidly in a rapidly expanding economy (the 1940s) than in an economy not living up to its potential (the latter part of the 1950s). Full employment, tight labor markets, high rates of growth are imperatives. They mean jobs, employer training programs, upgrading of labor, relaxation of undesirable restrictive hiring practices. I contend that the Negro will fare better in a redistribution of the fruits of progress than in a battle with others over the spoils of war.

This strikes close to and is also true for the issue often posed as "preferential treatment." Preferential treatment is not a wholly new concept on the American scene. In a very real sense we have witnessed it for decades—for whites. Separate and *unequal* schools, favoritism in hiring and employment, restrictive housing practices—often these were preferential treatment based on race. Universities have admitted less qualified students who were the sons of alumni, or who played band instruments at football games between groups of (other) preferentially treated students. Government expenditure (and tax) policy has given preference (some desirable—the War on Poverty; some undesirable—tax exemption of interest on state and local bonds). It is clear that preferential treatment can mean many different things and can take many different forms. The fact that it did exist in the past does not in itself mean that it should exist in the future. But it does suggest that it is not something completely new, to be rejected simply because it has not previously been used.

Attitudes to the phrase "preferential treatment" can vary with the policy that it calls to mind. Some may favor compensatory or supplemental educational programs and relaxed admission standards by universities but oppose preferential hiring policies by private employers. Some may favor programs to assist the Negro to attain required levels (via tutorial programs, on-the-job training, retraining, summer educational programs) but oppose preference except through such "compensatory" programs. Some may feel preference means assistance; others may feel it implies lowering of standards. And persons may disagree on the amount of preference to be granted: If assistance, how much? If relaxation of standards, how far? Does preference mean filling a vacancy with a Negro rather than a white when they are equal in all relevant respects, when the Negro is only a little less qualified, when he is substantially less qualified? Does preference mean extra dollars for Negro schools (how many dollars); does it mean extra training and upgrading programs (if so how many)?

Preferential treatment programs can be best discussed and evaluated as specific programs on their individual merits, each with its own costs, each with its own benefits. But all such programs share three things in common: (1) their goal is to speed progress—to leapfrog ahead (and in many areas discontinuities may require large, rapid, and dramatic gains rather than an ever so slow but steady movement, for the problems are complex and intertwined and psychology, motivation, and aspiration are part of them); (2) they are more readily accepted when they are designed to upgrade and remove disabilities or deficiencies rather than to "overlook" them; (3) they are more readily accepted when preference for some does not mean retrogression for others. Specific proposals should be evaluated in the light of these considerations. If this is done we may well find disagreement over words translated into agreement over policies.

We paint tomorrow's picture today. Much of the outline was given to us by yesterday's generation, but that rough sketch can be altered and enriched. We—the Negro and the white—are not captives of our yesterdays. Perhaps in years to come such essays will be written not by economists but by economic historians.

REFERENCES

1. Gunnar Myrdal, *An American Dilemma* (New York, 1944), p. xviii.
2. Data for 1920 and for persons aged twenty-five to twenty-nine from John K. Folger and Charles B. Nam, "Educational Trends from Census Data," *Demography*, Vol. 1, No. 1 (1964), pp. 247–57.

Capitalism and Discrimination

MILTON FRIEDMAN

*This essay was originally a chapter of Friedman's controversial
book,* Capitalism and Freedom.

IT IS A STRIKING historical fact that the development of captialism
has been accompanied by a major reduction in the extent to
which particular religious, racial, or social groups have operated
under special handicaps in respect of their economic activities;
have, as the saying goes, been discriminated against. The substitution of contract arrangements for status arrangements was
the first step toward the freeing of the serfs in the Middle Ages.
The preservation of Jews through the Middle Ages was possible
because of the existence of a market sector in which they could
operate and maintain themselves despite official persecution.
Puritans and Quakers were able to migrate to the New World
because they could accumulate the funds to do so in the market
despite disabilities imposed on them in other aspects of their life.
The Southern states after the Civil War took many measures to
impose legal restrictions on Negroes. One measure which was
never taken on any scale was the establishment of barriers to
the ownership of either real or personal property. The failure to
impose such barriers clearly did not reflect any special concern to
avoid restrictions on Negroes. It reflected, rather, a basic belief
in private property which was so strong that it overrode the desire to discriminate against Negroes. The maintenance of the
general rules of private property and of capitalism have been a
major source of opportunity for Negroes and have permitted
them to make greater progress than they otherwise could have
made. To take a more general example, the preserves of discrimination in any society are the areas that are most monopolistic
in character, whereas discrimination against groups of particular color or religion is least in those areas where there is the
greatest freedom of competition.

. . . One of the paradoxes of experience is that, in spite of this historical evidence, it is precisely the minority groups that have frequently furnished the most vocal and most numerous advocates of fundamental alterations in a capitalist society. They have tended to attribute to capitalism the residual restrictions they experience rather than to recognize that the free market has been the major factor enabling these restrictions to be as small as they are.

A free market separates economic efficiency from irrelevant characteristics. . . . The purchaser of bread does not know whether it was made from wheat grown by a white man or a Negro, by a Christian or a Jew. In consequence, the producer of wheat is in a position to use resources as effectively as he can, regardless of what the attitudes of the community may be toward the color, the religion, or other characteristics of the people he hires. Furthermore, and perhaps more important, there is an economic incentive in a free market to separate economic efficiency from other characteristics of the individual. A businessman or an entrepreneur who expresses preferences in his business activities that are not related to productive efficiency is at a disadvantage compared to other individuals who do not. Such an individual is in effect imposing higher costs on himself than are other individuals who do not have such preferences. Hence, in a free market they will tend to drive him out.

This same phenomenon is of much wider scope. It is often taken for granted that the person who discriminates against others because of their race, religion, color, or whatever, incurs no costs by doing so but simply imposes costs on others. This view is on a par with the very similar fallacy that a country does not hurt itself by imposing tariffs on the products of other countries. Both are equally wrong. The man who objects to buying from or working alongside a Negro, for example, thereby limits his range of choice. He will generally have to pay a higher price for what he buys or receive a lower return for his work. Or, put the other way, those of us who regard color of skin or religion as irrelevant can buy some things more cheaply as a result.

As these comments perhaps suggest, there are real problems in defining and interpreting discrimination. The man who exercises discrimination pays a price for doing so. He is, as it were, "buying" what he regards as a "product." It is hard to see that discrimination can have any meaning other than a "taste" of others that one does not share. We do not regard it as "discrimination"—or at least not in the same invidious sense—if an individual is willing to pay a higher price to listen to one singer than to another, although we do if he is willing to pay a higher price to have services rendered to him by a person of one color than by a in the one case we share the taste, and in the other case we do not. Is there any difference in principle between the taste that leads a householder to prefer an attractive servant to an ugly one and the taste that leads another to prefer a Negro to a white or a white to a Negro, except that we sympathize and agree with the one taste and may not with the other? I do not mean to say that all tastes are equally good. On the contrary, I believe strongly that the color of a man's skin or the religion of his parents is, by itself, no reason to treat him differently; that a man should be judged by what he is and what he does and not by these external characteristics. I deplore what seem to me the prejudice and narrowness of outlook of those whose tastes differ from mine in this respect and I think the less of them for it. But in a society based on free discussion, the appropriate recourse is for me to seek to persuade them that their tastes are bad and that they should change their views and their behavior, not to use coercive power to enforce my tastes and my attitudes on others.

FAIR EMPLOYMENT PRACTICES LEGISLATION

Fair employment practice commissions that have the task of preventing "discrimination" in employment by reason of race, color, or religion have been established in a number of states. Such legislation clearly involves interference with the freedom of individuals to enter into voluntary contracts with one another. It subjects any such contract to approval or disapproval by the state. Thus it is directly an interference with freedom of the kind that we would object to in most other contexts. Moreover, as is true with most other interferences with freedom, the individuals subjected to the law may well not be those whose actions even the proponents of the law wish to control.

For example, consider a situation in which there are grocery stores serving a neighborhood inhabited by people who have a strong aversion to being waited on by Negro clerks. Suppose one of the grocery stores has a vacancy for a clerk and the first applicant qualified in other respects happens to be a Negro. Let us suppose that as a result of the law the store is required to hire him. The effect of this action will be to reduce the business done by this store and to impose losses on the owner. If the preference of the community is strong enough, it may even cause the store to close. When the owner of the store hires white clerks in preference to Negroes in the absence of the law, he may not be expressing any preference or prejudice or taste of his own. He may simply be transmitting the tastes of the community. He is, as it were, producing the services for the consumers that the consumers are willing to pay for. Nonetheless, he is harmed, and indeed may be the only one harmed appreciably, by a law which prohibits him from engaging in this activity, that is, prohibits him from pandering to the tastes of the community for having a white rather than a Negro clerk. The consumers, whose preferences the law is intended to curb, will be affected substantially only to the extent that the number of stores is limited and hence they must pay higher prices because one store has gone out of business. This analysis can be generalized. In a very large fraction of cases, employers are transmitting the preference of either their customers or their other employees when they adopt employment policies that treat factors irrelevant to technical physical productivity as relevant to employment. Indeed, employers typically have an incentive, as noted earlier, to try to find ways of getting around the preferences of their consumers or of their employees if such preferences impose higher costs upon them.

The proponents of FEPC argue that interference with the freedom of individuals to enter into contracts with one another with respect to employment is justified because the individual who refuses to hire a Negro instead of a white, when both are equally qualified in terms of physical productive capacity, is harming others, namely, the particular color or religious group whose employment opportunity is limited in the process. This argument involves a serious confusion between two very different kinds of harm. One kind is the positive harm that one individual does another by physical force, or by forcing him to enter into a contract without his consent. An obvious example is the man who hits another over the head with a blackjack. A less obvious example is stream pollution. . . . The second kind is the negative harm that occurs when two individuals are unable to find mutually acceptable contracts, as when I am unwilling to buy something that someone wants to sell me and therefore make him worse off than he would be if I bought the item. If the community at large has a preference for blues singers rather than for opera singers, they are certainly increasing the economic well-being of the first relative to the second. If a potential blues singer can find employment and a potential opera singer cannot, this simply means that the blues singer is rendering services which the community regards as worth paying for wheareas the potential opera singer is not. The potential opera singer is "harmed" by the community's taste. He would be better off and the blues singer "harmed" if the tastes were the reverse. Clearly, this kind of harm does not involve any involuntary exchange or an imposition of costs or granting of benefits to third parties. There is a strong case for using government to prevent one person from imposing positive harm, which is to say, to prevent coercion. There is no case whatsoever for using government to avoid the negative kind of "harm." On the contrary, such government intervention reduces freedom and limits voluntary cooperation.

FEPC legislation involves the acceptance of a principle that proponents would find abhorrent in almost every other application. If it is appropriate for the state to say that individuals may not discriminate in employment because of color or race or religion, then it is equally appropriate for the state, provided a majority can be found to vote that way, to say that individuals must discriminate in employment on the basis of color, race, or religion. The Hitler Nuremberg laws and the laws in the Southern states imposing special disabilities upon Negroes are both examples of laws similar in principle to FEPC. Opponents of such laws who are in favor of FEPC cannot argue that there is anything wrong with them in principle, that they involve a kind of state action that ought not to be permitted. They can only argue that the particular criteria used are irrelevant. They can only seek to persuade other men that they should use other criteria instead of these.

If one takes a broad sweep of history and looks at the kind of things that the majority will be persuaded of if each individual case is to be decided on its merits rather than as part of a general principle, there can be little doubt that the effect on a widespread acceptance of the appropriateness of government action in this area would be extremely undersirable, even from the point of view of those who at the moment favor FEPC. If, at the moment, the proponents of FEPC are in a position to make their views effective, it is only because of a constitutional and federal situation in which a regional majority in one part of the country may be in a position to impose its views on a majority in another part of the country.

As a general rule, any minority that counts on specific majority action to defend its interests is short-sighted in the extreme. Acceptance of a general self-denying ordinance applying to a class of cases may inhibit specific majorities from exploiting specific minorities. In the absence of such a self-denying ordinance, majorities can surely be counted on to use their power to give effect to their preferences, or if you will, prejudices, not to protect minorities from the prejudices of majorities.

To put the matter in another and perhaps more striking way, consider an individual who believes that the present pattern of tastes is undesirable and who believes that Negroes have less opportunity than he would like to see them have. Suppose he puts his beliefs into practice by always choosing the Negro applicant for a job whenever there are a number of applicants more or less equally qualified in other respects. Under present circumstances should he be prevented from doing so? Clearly the logic of the FEPC is that he should be.

The counterpart to fair employment in the area where these principles have perhaps been worked out more than any other, namely, the area of speech, is "fair speech" rather than free speech. In this respect the position of the American Civil Liberties Union seems utterly contradictory. It favors both free speech and fair employment laws. One way to state the justification for free speech is that we do not believe that it is desirable that momentary majorities decide what at any moment shall be regarded as appropriate speech. We want a free market in ideas, so that ideas get a chance to win majority or near-unanimous acceptance, even if initially held only by a few. Precisely the same considerations apply to employment or more generally to the market for goods and services. Is it any more desirable that momentary majorities decide what characteristics are relevant to employment than what speech is appropriate? Indeed, can a free market in ideas long be maintained if a free market in goods and services is destroyed? The ACLU will fight to the death to protect the right of a racist to preach on a street corner the doctrine of racial segregation. But it will favor putting him in jail if he acts on his principles by refusing to hire a Negro for a particular job.

As already stressed, the appropriate recourse of those of us who believe that a particular criterion such as color is irrelevant is to persuade our fellows to be of like mind, not to use the coercive power of the state to force them to act in accordance with our principles. Of all groups, the ACLU should be the first both to recognize and proclaim that this is so.

RIGHT-TO-WORK LAWS

Some states have passed so-called "right-to-work" laws. These are laws which make it illegal to require membership in a union as a condition of employment.

The principles involved in right-to-work laws are identical with those involved in FEPC. Both interfere with the freedom of the employment contract, in the one case by specifying that a particular color or religion cannot be made a condition of employment; in the other, that membership in a union cannot be. Despite the identity of principle, there is almost 100 percent divergence of views with respect to the two laws. Almost all who favor FEPC oppose right to work; almost all who favor right to work oppose FEPC. As a liberal, I am opposed to both, as I am equally to laws outlawing the so-called "yellow-dog" contract (a contract making nonmembership in a union a condition of employment).

Given competition among employers and employees, there seems no reason why employers should not be free to offer any terms they want to their employees. In some cases employers find that employees prefer to have part of their remuneration take the form of amenities such as baseball fields or play facilities or better rest facilities rather than cash. Employers then find that it is more profitable to offer these facilities as part of their employment contract rather than to offer higher cash wages. Similarly, employers may offer pension plans, or require participation in pension plans, and the like. None of this involves any interference with the freedom of individuals to find employment. It simply reflects an attempt by employers to make the characteristics of the job suitable and attractive to employees. So long as there are many employers, all employees who have particular kinds of wants will be able to satisfy them by finding employment with corresponding employers. Under competitive conditions the same thing would be true with respect to the closed shop. If in fact some employees would prefer to work in firms that have a closed shop and others in firms that have an open shop, there would develop different forms of employment contracts, some having the one provision, others the other provision.

As a practical matter, of course, there are some important differences between FEPC and right to work. The differences are the presence of monopoly in the form of union organizations on the employee side and the presence of federal legislation in respect of labor unions. It is doubtful that in a competitive labor market, it would in fact ever be profitable for employers to offer a closed shop as a condition of employment. Whereas unions may frequently be found without any strong monopoly power on the side of labor, a closed shop almost never is. It is almost always a symbol of monopoly power.

The coincidence of a closed shop and labor monopoly is not an argument for a right-to-work law. It is an argument for action to eliminate monopoly power regardless of the particular forms and manifestations which it takes. It is an argument for more effective and widespread antitrust action in the labor field.

Another special feature that is important in practice is the conflict between federal and state law and the existence at the moment of a federal law which applies to all the states and which leaves a loophole for the individual state only through the passage of a right-to-work law. The optimum solution would be to have the federal law revised. The difficulty is that no individual state is in a position to bring this about and yet people within an individual state might wish to have a change in the legislation governing union organization within their state. The right-to-work law may be the only effective way in which this can be done and therefore the lesser of evils. Partly, I suppose, because I am inclined to believe that a right-to-work law will not in and of itself have any great effect on the monopoly power of the unions, I do not accept this justification for it. The practical arguments seem to me much too weak to outweigh the objection of principle.

SEGREGATION IN SCHOOLING

Segregation in schooling raises a particular problem not covered by the previous comments for one reason only. The reason is that schooling is, under present circumstances, primarily operated and administered by government. This means that government must make an explicit decision. It must either enforce segregation or enforce integration. Both seem to me bad solutions. Those of us who believe that color of skin is an irrelevant characteristic and that it is desirable for all to recognize this, yet who also believe in individual freedom, are therefore faced with a dilemma. If one must choose between the evils of enforced segregation or enforced integration, I myself would find it impossible not to choose integration.

. . . The appropriate solution is to eliminate government operation of the schools and permit parents to choose the kind of school they want their children to attend. In addition, of course, we should all of us, insofar as we possibly can, try by behavior and speech to foster the growth of attitudes and opinions that would lead mixed schools to become the rule and segregated schools the rare exception.

If a proposal like the preceding were adopted, it would permit a variety of schools to develop, some all white, some all Negro, some mixed. It would permit the transition from one collection of schools to another—hopefully to mixed schools—to be gradual as community attitudes changed. It would avoid the harsh political conflict that has been doing so much to raise social tensions and disrupt the community. It would in this special area, as the market does in general, permit cooperation without conformity.

The state of Virginia has adopted a plan having many features in common with that outlined in the preceding. Though adopted for the purpose of avoiding compulsory integration, I predict that the ultimate effects of the law will be very different—after all, the difference between result and intention is one of the primary justifications of a free society; it is desirable to let men follow the bent of their own interests because there is no way of predicting where they will come out. Indeed, even in the early stages there have been surprises. I have been told that one of the first requests for a voucher to finance a change of school was by a parent transferring a child from a segregated to an integrated school. The transfer was requested not for this purpose but simply because the integrated school happened to be the better school educationally. Looking further ahead, if the voucher system is not abolished, Virginia will provide an experiment to test the conclusions of the preceding chapter. If those conclusions are right, we should see a flowering of the schools available in Virginia, with an increase in their diversity, a substantial if not spectacular rise in the quality of the leading schools, and a later rise in the quality of the rest under the impetus of the leaders.

On the other side of the picture, we should not be so naïve as to suppose that deep-seated values and beliefs can be uprooted in short measure by law. I live in Chicago. Chicago has no law compelling segregation. Its laws require integration. Yet in fact the public schools of Chicago are probably as thoroughly segregated as the schools of most Southern cities. There is almost no doubt at all that if the Virginia system were introduced in Chicago, the result would be an appreciable decrease in segregation, and a great widening in the opportunities available to the ablest and most ambitious Negro youth.

The Economic Role of Women

COUNCIL OF ECONOMIC ADVISERS

*This discussion of the economic role of women in the labor mar-
ket originally appeared in the 1973 Annual Report of the President's Council of Economic Advisers.*

ONE OF THE MOST important changes in the American economy
in this century has been the increase in the proportion of women
who work outside the home. This increase is the most striking
aspect of the expansion of the role of women in the economy.

The addition of millions of women to the labor force has contributed substantially to the increase of total output. This is most
obvious if we focus attention on the output that is measured
and included in the Gross National Product (GNP). But even if
we subtract from the contribution of working women to the
GNP the value of the work they would have done at home, there
has been an addition to total output. Most of the benefits of this
additional output accrue to the women who produce it, and to
their families. There are, however, also direct benefits to the
society at large, including the taxes paid on the women's
earnings.

Concern is sometimes expressed that the increase in women
in the labor force will reduce the employment opportunities for
men and raise their unemployment. There is no reason to think
that would happen and there is no sign that it has happened.
The work to be done is not a fixed total. As more women enter
employment and earn incomes they or their families buy more
goods and services which men and women are employed to produce. A sudden surge of entrants into the labor force might cause
difficulties of adjustment and, consequently, unemployment, but
the entry of women into the labor force has not been of that
character.

Women work outside the home for the same reasons as men.
The basic reason is to get the income that can be earned by
working. Whether—for either men or women—work is done out

of necessity or by choice is a question of definition. If working out of necessity means working in order to sustain biologically necessary conditions of life, probably a small proportion of all the hours of work done in the United States, by men or women, is necessary. If working out of necessity means working in order to obtain a standard of living which is felt by the worker to be desirable, probably almost all of the work done by both men and women is necessary. The Employment Act of 1946 sets forth a goal of "maximum employment." We understand that to mean employment of those who want to work without regard to whether their employment is, by some definition, necessary. This goal applies equally to men and to women. The Act also sets forth a goal of "maximum production." We understand the meaning of that goal which is relevant to the present context to be that people should be able to work in the employments in which they will be most productive. That also applies equally to men and women.

Although the goals apply equally to men and women, some of the obstacles to their achievement apply especially to women. Women have gained much more access to market employment than they used to have, but they have not gained full equality within the market in the choice of jobs, opportunities for advancement, and other matters related to employment and compensation. To some extent the cause of this discrepancy is direct discrimination. But it is also the result of more subtle and complex factors originating in cultural patterns that have grown up in most societies through the centuries. In either case, because the possibilities open to women are restricted, they are not always free to contribute a full measure of earning to their families, to develop their talents fully, or to help achieve the nation's goal of "maximum production." . . .

PARTICIPATION IN THE LABOR FORCE

In 1900 about 20 percent of all women were in the work force (Table 1). In the succeeding decades this percentage hardly increased, reaching about 25 percent by 1940. With World War II, however, the movement rapidly accelerated, and by 1972 the percentage of women 16 years and older in the work force had risen to 43.8. Single women and women widowed, divorced, or

TABLE 1. *Women in the Labor Force, Selected Years, 1900–1972*

Year	Women in labor force (thousands)	Women in labor force as percentage of	
		Total labor force	All women of working age
1900	5,114	18.1	20.4
1910	7,889	20.9	25.2
1920	8,430	20.4	23.3
1930	10,679	22.0	24.3
1940	12,845	24.3	25.4
1945	19,270	29.6	35.7
1950	18,412	28.8	33.9
1955	20,584	30.2	35.7
1960	23,272	32.3	37.8
1965	26,232	34.0	39.3
1970	31,560	36.7	43.4
1972	33,320	37.4	43.8

separated have always had higher labor-force participation rates than married women living with their husbands. By 1950, the participation of women in the two former groups had already reached levels close to those of today. Thus, the upward trend in labor-force participation since World War II has been due almost entirely to the changed behavior of married women (Table 2). The first to respond were the more mature married women beyond the usual childbearing years. More recently there has also been a sharp upturn in the labor-force participation of younger married women.

The record for men has tended to run in the opposite direction. A secular reduction in time spent in paid work over men's lifetimes has taken place: A man spends more years at school and enters the labor force later than formerly; he retires earlier, works fewer hours a week, and has longer vacations. Of course these changes have also affected women, but for them the increase in years worked has far outweighed the other work-reducing factors.

In one very important respect, however, the working life patterns of men and women have not merged. The typical man can expect to be in the labor force continuously, for an unbroken block of some 40 years between leaving school and retirement. Of men in the 25–54 year age group, 95.2 percent were in the labor force in 1972. For most women, this continuity in participation is the exception rather than the rule.

TABLE 2. *Labor-force Participation Rates of Women by Marital Status and Age, 1950, 1960, and 1972*

(*percent* [1])

Marital status and year	Total	Age					
		Under 20 years	20–24 years	25–34 years	35–44 years	45–64 years	65 years and over
Single:							
1950	50.5	26.3	74.9	84.6	83.6	70.6	23.8
1960	44.1	25.3	73.4	79.9	79.7	75.1	21.6
1972	54.9	41.9	69.9	84.7	71.5	71.0	19.0
Married, husband present:							
1950	23.8	24.0	28.5	23.8	28.5	21.8	6.4
1960	30.5	25.3	30.0	27.7	36.2	34.2	5.9
1972	41.5	39.0	48.5	41.3	48.6	44.2	7.3
Widowed, divorced, or separated:							
1950	37.8	(2)	45.5	62.3	65.4	50.2	8.8
1960	40.0	37.3	54.6	55.5	67.4	58.3	11.0
1972	40.1	44.6	57.6	62.1	71.7	61.1	9.8

1. Labor force as percentage of noninstitutional population in group specified.
2. Not available.

The historical pattern · What are the causal factors that induced women to enter the labor force? One might have expected that the strong increases in husbands' real incomes which occurred during the period would have provided an incentive to women not to enter the labor force. This seeming puzzle is resolved however, when one considers that by entering the labor force women did not leave a life of leisure for work, but rather changed from one kind of work, work at home, to another kind of work, work in the market. The incentive for women to make this dramatic occupational change came from several developments which made paid work outside the home the increasingly more profitable alternative.

Rapidly rising earnings and expanded job opportunities for women gave a strong impetus to the change. The expansion of job opportunities for women was undoubtedly influenced by the expansion of the service sector of the economy, where employment increased by 77 percent from 1950 to 1970, compared to the increase of 26 percent in the goods-producing industrial sector over the same period. Women have always been more heavily represented in services than in industry, since the service sector offers more white-collar employment and provides more opportunities for part-time work, an especially important feature for women with small children. On the other hand, the increasing supply of women workers perhaps itself contributed to the rapid expansion in the service sector.

The increase in women's educational attainments has also helped to raise the amount they can earn by working. Education may make women more productive in the home, that is, more efficient housekeepers, consumers, and mothers, but education appears to increase still more their productivity in work outside the home. Women with more education earn more, and they are more likely than less educated women to seek work in the market.

Because life expectancy has increased considerably over the century (and more for women than for men), and because most women complete their childbearing at a younger age, women can look forward with more certainty to a longer uninterrupted span of years in the labor force. This lengthening of a woman's expected working life is significant because it increases her return on her investment in training and education: the greater the number of years in which to collect the return the greater is the return.

These increases in the income a woman could potentially earn meant essentially that time spent producing goods and services at home was coming at a higher and higher cost in terms of the income foregone by not working in the market. It made sense then to buy available capital equipment (such as washing machines) which would substitute for some of the housewife's time and free her to go to work. And changes in technology which lowered the cost and increased the array of time-saving devices facilitated the substitution.

The most difficult home responsibility to find a good substitute for is child care; and, although the labor-force participation of women with children under six years has increased from 12 percent in 1950 to 30 percent in 1971, child-rearing is probably

PARTICIPATION RATE (PERCENT)*

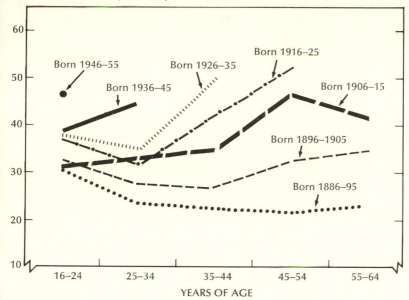

YEARS OF AGE

* Total Labor Force as Percentage of Total Noninstitutional Population in Group Specified.

the major factor causing some women to interrupt and others to curtail their careers.

The long-term decline in the average number of children in the family has undoubtedly had a strong influence on the proportion of women entering the labor force. Advances in birth control techniques permit parents not only to reduce the number of births but also to control their timing to suit a mother's working career. Declines in infant and child mortality may also have encouraged a reduction in births by increasing the parents' expectation that all their children would survive to adulthood. On the other hand, reductions in family size may themselves be influenced by the desire of women to work.

Childbearing has a very noticeable effect on the patterns of women's labor-force participation by age. Based on census data, Chart 1 traces the lifetime changes in labor force participation by groups of women born at different times, the earliest group consisting of women born between 1886 and 1895. The chart therefore simulates the actual work history of particular cohorts of women followed longitudinally. According to this chart, the various forces in the economy that have induced women to work have generally had a more powerful effect on women beyond the childbearing ages than on younger groups. Those increases in labor-force participation that have occurred for groups of women reaching the childbearing ages of 20–34 years have been closely associated with declining fertility rates. Thus labor-force participation for the group reaching 25–34 years increased substantially from 1930 to 1940, and again between 1960 and 1970, while there was a decline between 1940 and 1950 in the participation of those reaching this age group—the baby-boom mothers. Whether the young women now in their twenties have simply postponed having children and will later drop out of the labor force or whether many will continue to work, choosing to have small families or remain childless is, of course, a question of great interest.

The working woman today · Although the decisions of individual women to work outside the home are undoubtedly based on many different factors, there are some economic factors which seem to be of overriding importance. The necessity to support oneself or others is one obvious reason and, not surprisingly, adult single women and women who have been separated from husbands or widowed are highly likely to work.

The increase in earnings opportunities, which proved to be such a powerful factor influencing the secular growth of women's participation in the labor force, is a similarly powerful factor influencing the pattern of women's participation at any given time. Thus, education and other training which affect the amount a woman can earn are strongly related to women's work patterns. The importance of education is such that, whether a woman is single, married, or separated, the more education she has, the more likely she is to work. One striking exception to this pattern is that, among mothers of children under six years old, there is scarcely any relation between education and labor force participation. Thus, the rearing of children of preschool age causes all women, regardless of education, to curtail their work outside the home. However, the drop in participation during this child-rearing period is most pronounced for highly educated women who in other circumstances have much higher participation rates.

Although for most women the childbearing period has been

reduced, childbearing still means an interruption of outside work. A longitudinal survey of the lifelong work experience of women indicates that among all women who were 30–44 years old in 1967, only 7 percent had worked at least six months out of every year since leaving school. Among married women with children the proportion was still lower, dropping to 3 percent. By contrast, 30 percent of childless married women in the same group had worked at least six months out of every year. Information on job tenure collected by the Bureau of Labor Statistics illustrates much the same phenomenon. As of January 1968, continuous employment in the current job came to 2.4 years (the median) for women and 4.8 years for men. Job tenure increases with age for both men and women. At ages 45 and over the median was 12.7 years for men and 6.6 years for women. Since women tend to change jobs less frequently than men, their shorter time spent on any given job is the result of a higher propensity to leave the labor force at least temporarily. In 1964 a survey of women who had dropped out of the labor force in 1962 or 1963 and had not yet reentered was undertaken by the Labor Department in an effort to find out why they had left. Pregnancy was most frequently cited as the primary reason— by 74 percent of the 18- to 24-year-olds and 56 percent of the 25- to 34-year-olds.

Among married women, husband's income does not have a very pronounced effect on work patterns. The median annual income of husbands with working wives was $8,070 in 1971 compared to $8,330 for husbands of wives not in the labor force. Only when husbands' incomes reach the $10,000 and over category does wives' participation decline to any noticeable extent. However, many other things vary with husbands' incomes, such as wives' education and age as well as family size. These other factors are sufficiently important to obscure the simple relation between husband's income and a wife's tendency to work. It should be noted, however, that during a time of hardship, such as when a husband experiences a prolonged spell of unemployment, wives who usually do not work may be compelled to work. Thus, the labor-force participation of women with unemployed husbands is generally above that of women with employed husbands.

Although the probability that a black woman will work seems to vary with education and presence of children in much the same way as it does for all women, there is one very striking difference: the labor-force participation of black women is higher. Particularly pronounced differences are observed when the comparison of labor-force participation is confined to married women living with their husbands. In March 1971, about 53 percent of black wives were in the labor force compared to 40 percent of white wives. One important reason why this difference prevails may be that the earnings of black wives are closer to their husbands' than is the case among white married couples. In 1971 black married women who worked year-round, full-time earned 73 percent as much as black married men who worked year-round, full-time. Among whites the percentage was only 51 percent. Behind these relationships is the fact that black men earn considerably less than white men, while black women's earnings are much closer to white women's earnings.

UNEMPLOYMENT

Women have generally experienced more unemployment than men and this differential has been more pronounced in recent years (Table 3). However, the source of women's unemployment differs from that of men's, and this makes a comparison of unemployment differences more complex than might appear.

Some of the difference arises from the way people are classified in our unemployment statistics. A person with a job is not classified as unemployed even though he or she may be searching for another job. However, work at home is not counted as a job. Thus, a woman who may in a real sense be clearly employed in the home while she searches for a job, will be counted as unemployed, unlike the man who searches while on his job.

Most adult men are continuously in the labor force and therefore become unemployed because they have either quit or lost their jobs (Table 4). For women, the picture is different: labor-force participation is frequently interrupted, sometimes for several years, but sometimes just for several weeks during the year. Thus, although 59.8 percent of the women 24–54 years old were in the labor force at one time or another during 1971, only 38.2 percent were in the labor force for 50–52 weeks during the year. This high rate of labor-force turnover generates unemployment, and it is not surprising to find that in both the tight labor

TABLE 3. *Unemployment Rates by Sex and Age,*
Selected Years, 1956–72

(*percent* [1])

Sex and age	1956	1961	1965	1969	1972
All workers	4.1	6.7	4.5	3.5	5.6
Men	3.8	6.4	4.0	2.8	4.9
16–19 years	11.1	17.1	14.1	11.4	15.9
20–24 years	6.9	10.8	6.4	5.1	9.2
25–54 years	3.0	5.1	2.7	1.6	3.1
55 years and over	3.5	5.7	3.3	1.9	3.3
Women	4.9	7.2	5.5	4.7	6.6
16–19 years	11.2	16.3	15.7	13.3	16.7
20–24 years	6.3	9.8	7.3	6.3	9.3
25–54 years	4.1	6.2	4.3	3.5	4.9
55 years and over	3.3	4.4	2.8	2.2	3.4

1. Unemployment as percentage of civilian labor force in group specified.

TABLE 4. *Distribution of Unemployment of Adult Men and*
Women by Reason for Unemployment, 1969 and 1972

(*percent*)

Reason for unemployment	Men 20 years and over		Women 20 years and over	
	1969	1972	1969	1972
Total unemployment	100.0	100.0	100.0	100.0
Separated from a job	74.8	75.3	49.9	55.7
Job losers	57.8	62.6	33.0	39.4
Job leavers	17.0	12.7	16.8	16.3
Labor force entrants	25.2	24.6	50.2	44.3
Reentrants	22.4	21.6	44.8	39.4
New entrants	2.8	3.1	5.5	4.9
Unemployment rate	2.1	4.0	3.7	5.4

NOTE: Detail may not add to totals because of rounding.
SOURCE: Department of Labor, Bureau of Labor Statistics.

market of 1969 and the looser labor market of 1972 a considerable portion of unemployed women were labor-force entrants (Table 4). People entering or reentering the labor force tend, however, to be unemployed for relatively short periods, and this is one of the reasons why the duration of unemployment is in general shorter for women than for men (Table 5).

In order to know what significance to attach to the observation that the greater unemployment of women appears to be related

TABLE 5. *Unemployment of Adult Men and Women by Duration and Reason, 1972*

| | | Percentage of total unemployment | |
Sex, age, and reason	Total unemployment (thousands)	Unemployment of less than 5 weeks	Unemployment of 15 weeks and over
Men 20 years and over	1,928	37.0	31.6
Lost last job	1,207	33.6	35.3
Left last job	245	44.9	24.9
Reentered labor force	416	41.7	25.4
Never worked before	59	39.0	28.8
Women 20 years and over	1,610	48.4	22.8
Lost last job	635	35.6	33.4
Left last job	262	50.0	19.2
Reentered labor force	635	59.8	14.4
Never worked before	79	55.7	16.5

NOTE: Detail may not add to totals because of rounding.

to their greater labor-force turnover, it is of course necessary to know more about the causes of the turnover. Some have stressed that excessive labor-force turnover indicates a poor job market. According to this view, women drop out of the labor market because lack of opportunities has discouraged them from continuing the search. Evidence for this point of view is cited from Labor Department surveys, which indicate that some of those women out of the labor force are there because they do not believe they could find work. In 1972, 525,000 women or 1.2 percent of those out of the labor force were reported in this category.

Another school of thought, however, stresses that the labor-force turnover of women and the unemployment it generates is largely induced by factors external to the current labor market, such as the uneven pressures of home responsibilities. Several kinds of evidence support this point of view. Unemployment among women appears to be related to the nature of home responsibilities. For example, in 1971 the unemployment rate for married women with children under 3 years was 11.7 percent, compared to the rate of 4.5 percent for married women with no children under 18 years. Moreover, on numerous surveys women cite pregnancy, home responsibilities, or husband's relocation as primary reasons for leaving the job or the labor force.

It would of course be interesting to know more about the unemployment experience of women who do remain continuously in the labor force. Some evidence from the Labor Department's longitudinal survey indicates that women who were in the labor force in both 1967 and 1969 had considerably lower unemployment in 1969 than those who were in the labor force in 1969 but not in 1967. The unemployment rate in 1969 for the group who were also in the labor force two years previously was 2.9 percent, compared to the rate of 6.9 percent for the women who were in the labor force only in 1969. However, this was still above the rate of 2.1 percent for men 20 years old and over in 1969, as measured by the household survey.

Although movement in and out of the labor force is probably the most important factor leading to higher unemployment for women compared to men, two other factors seem to be important. Women with less time on a job and in whom the employer has made negligible training investments are more vulnerable to layoffs. Finally, one additional factor which doubtless contributes to unemployment of married women is the difficulty in maximizing employment opportunities for both the husband and the wife. A wife seldom is free to migrate to wherever her own prospects are best.

It is important to emphasize, because the point is often misunderstood, that to explain the unemployment of women is not to excuse it or belittle it or to place blame on the women who are unemployed. The unemployment of women who seek work is costly, to themselves, their families, and the nation. Our goal should be to reduce this unemployment wherever that can be done by means which are not themselves more costly. Some unemployment entails more loss for the workers involved and to the economy as a whole than other; some is more amenable to correction by the persons directly affected than other unemployment. But these distinctions do not run along sex lines.

The widening in the reported male-female unemployment differential · During the 1960s the differential in reported unemployment between women and men widened. Two factors may help to explain the change. The first has to do with changes in the unemployment survey questionnaire introduced in 1967.

Persons are classified as unemployed if they have not worked during the survey week, were available to work during the survey week, and had made specific efforts to find a job such as looking in the "want-ads" section of the newspaper or going to an employment agency. Prior to 1967 the period of jobseeking efforts was not specified, and it is believed that many respondents interpreted the question narrowly to mean that one had to have looked for a job in the week just prior to the survey. In 1967 the unemployment question was changed by specifying four weeks preceding the survey as the point of reference. Data from samples taken on both the old and new basis are available for 1966. In that year the unemployment rate for women aged 20 years or older was 0.4 percentage points higher on the new basis than on the old. This increase in the rate for women as a result of the change in the questionnaire has been interpreted as reflecting the likelihood that the jobseeking activities of women are more intermittent. As a result of lengthening the reference period to four weeks, persons who had briefly looked for work but who were not actively seeking work by the time of the survey week would be added to the unemployed under the new definition.

Although the reported unemployment of some men may also have been increased as a result of the effective lengthening of the unemployment reference period, other changes in the questionnaire in 1967, which were evidently unimportant for women, seemed to reduce the reported unemployment of men. Indeed these changes were of sufficient importance that the net effect was to lower the unemployment rate for men 20 years old and over by 0.3 percentage points. The unemployment rate for men was evidently lowered for two reasons: By a reclassification from unemployed to employed of persons absent from work because of a vacation or a labor dispute but at the same time looking for work; and by the fact that persons stating that they had given up the search for work were no longer counted as unemployed.

The 1966 samples indicate that as a result of the changes in the unemployment questionnaire, which increased the rate for women and lowered the rate for men, the reported male-female unemployment differential, comparing men and women 20 years old and over, increased from 1.3 percentage points to 2.0 percentage points. We cannot, of course, be sure that effects of the same precise magnitude have persisted ever since the new definitions were substituted in 1967. However, the definitional change has undoubtedly contributed to a wider unemployment differential since the late 1960s.

Another factor contributing to the widening of the unemployment differential may be the rapid increase in the labor force participation of women during the 1960s, since its effect was to increase the proportion of women entering or reentering the labor force, with an accompanying increase in unemployment.

EDUCATION AND THE OCCUPATIONAL DISTRIBUTION

Some of the hesitancy of women to enter or to stay in the labor force is undoubtedly the result of societally determined factors that restrict the possibilities open to them. The low representation of women in positions of responsibility is striking. Despite gradual gains, progress has not been sufficient to alter the picture significantly (Table 6). Exactly how much of this situation has been imposed on women because of prejudice and how much of it derives from a voluntary adjustment to a life divided between home responsibilities and work remains obscure. The existence of discriminatory barriers may discourage women from seeking the training or adopting the life style it would take to achieve a responsible and highly demanding job. On the other hand, women who expect to marry and have children and who also put their role at home first are subject to considerable uncertainty about their future attachment to the labor force. In the latter

TABLE 6. *Women as a Percentage of Persons in Several Professional and Managerial Occupations, 1910–1970*

(*percent*)

Occupational group	1910	1920	1930	1940	1950	1960	1970
Clergymen	0.6	1.4	2.2	2.4	4.0	2.3	2.9
College presidents, professors, and instructors [1]	18.9	30.2	31.9	26.5	23.2	24.2	28.2
Dentists	3.1	3.3	1.9	1.5	2.7	2.3	3.5
Editors and reporters	12.2	16.8	24.0	25.0	32.0	36.6	40.6
Engineers	(2)	(2)	(2)	.4	1.2	.8	1.6
Lawyers and judges	.5	1.4	2.1	2.5	3.5	3.5	4.9
Managers, manufacturing industries	1.7	3.1	3.2	4.3	6.4	7.1	6.3
Physicians	6.0	5.0	4.4	4.7	6.1	6.9	9.3

1. Data for 1920 and 1930 probably include some teachers in schools below collegiate rank. The Office of Education estimates the 1930 figure closer to 28 percent.

2. Less than one tenth of 1 percent.

case, incentives to train extensively for a career would be few; and, once such women started working, the restrictions imposed by home responsibilities could limit their ability to take a job requiring long hours or the intensive commitment that most high-status positions demand. At the same time, changes in the accepted social roles of men and women would alter current patterns if they changed women's expectations about their future in the labor force.

For whatever reasons, from school onward the career orientation of women differs strikingly from that of men. Most women do not have as strong a vocational emphasis in their schooling; and for those who do, the preparation is usually for a stereotyped "female" occupation.

Although the probability of graduating from high school has been somewhat greater for women than for men, it is less probable that a woman will complete college, and still less that she will enter graduate school. The representation of women consequently declines as they move upward through the stages of education beyond high school. In 1971, 50 percent of all high school graduates were women and 45 percent of first-year college students were women. During 1971 women earned 44 percent of the bachelor's degrees granted, 40 percent of the master's degrees, and 14 percent of the doctorates.

Even more striking are the differences in the courses taken. At both the undergraduate and advanced levels, women are heavily represented in English, languages, and fine arts—the more general cultural fields. They are poorly represented in disciplines having a strong vocational emphasis and promising a high pecuniary return. In 1970, 9.3 percent of the baccalaureates in business and 3.9 percent of the masters in business went to women. In the biological sciences, women had a larger share, taking about 30 percent of the bachelor's and master's degrees and 16 percent of the doctorates. But only 8.5 percent of the M.D.s and 5.6 percent of the law degrees went to women. Most of these percentages, low as they are, represent large gains from the preceding year.

The situation is quite different in the so-called women's occupations. In 1971 women received 74 percent of the B.A.s and 56 percent of the M.A.s given in education. In library science, which is even more firmly dominated by women, they received

82 percent of all degrees in 1971. And in nursing, 98 percent of all the degrees went to women.

It is not surprising, then, to find that women do not have anything like the same occupational distribution as men. Even within an educational level, significant differences remain in the distribution across broad occupational categories (Table 7). Although 77 percent of women college graduates in 1970 were in the professions, mostly as teachers, only 4.8 percent, compared to 20 percent for men, were classified as managers. At high school levels, the proportion of women working as skilled craftsmen is minuscule, although a substantial proportion of women are blue-collar workers in the lower paying operative categories.

. . . Although women are found in all occupations, the extent of occupational segregation by sex is large. In broad outline, this situation does not appear to have undergone any dramatic change between 1950 and 1970, although there are several examples of large increases in the proportion of women in less typically "female" occupations (for example, busdrivers, bartenders, and compositors and typesetters).

Casual observation of individual occupations cannot, of course, provide a comprehensive indication of whether the occupational distributions of men and women, involving numerous occupations, have moved closer together or further apart. To help answer this question, an index was constructed and calculated for 1960 and 1970 which reflects the difference (for 197 occupations) between the occupational distributions of men and women. The index displays a small move toward occupational similarity between 1960 and 1970. . . .

Another question of interest is whether the changes in the occupational distributions of men and women were in the direction of higher economic status and, if so, how far they went. Some insight into this question is obtained by calculating an index which reflects what earnings would have been in 1950, 1960, and 1970, if earnings were the same in all three years and only the occupational distributions changed. Median earnings for year-round, full-time workers in each of 11 broad occupational categories were used as the constant weights to calculate such an index. The results indicated that the occupational distributions of both men and women shifted in the direction of higher-earnings occupations from 1950 to 1960 and from 1960 to 1970. How-

TABLE 7. *Occupational Distribution of Employed Persons by Education and Sex, 1970* (percent)

Occupational groups	High school				College graduates	
	1–3 years		4 years			
	Men	Women	Men	Women	Men	Women
Total employed	100.0	100.0	100.0	100.0	100.0	100.0
Professional, technical, and kindred workers	2.8	3.6	7.6	7.1	58.9	77.4
Managers and proprietors	6.9	2.9	11.4	3.8	20.1	4.8
Salesworkers	5.6	10.2	7.5	8.1	8.6	2.3
Clerical and kindred workers	6.8	25.3	10.0	50.4	4.9	12.1
Craftsmen	25.6	2.4	26.4	1.8	3.3	0.4
Operatives	27.3	22.5	20.6	11.4	1.4	0.6
Nonfarm laborers	9.9	1.6	5.3	0.8	0.5	0.1
Farm laborers and foremen	1.9	0.6	0.9	0.3	0.2	0.1
Farmers and farm managers	2.2	0.2	2.9	0.2	0.8	0.1
Service workers excluding private household	10.8	25.4	7.5	14.5	1.4	1.9
Private household service workers	0.2	5.2	([1])	1.7	([1])	0.3

1. Less than one-tenth of 1 percent.

ever, in the earlier period men moved ahead in this respect faster than women while in the second period the changes were similar for both.

EARNINGS

In 1971 annual median earnings for women 14 years old and over were $2,986, or 40 percent of the median earnings of men. But women work fewer hours per week and fewer weeks per year. If the comparison is restricted to year-round, full-time workers, women's earnings are 60 percent of men's, that is, $5,593 compared to $9,399. An additional adjustment for differences in the average full-time workweek—full-time hours for men were about 10 percent higher than for women—brings the female-male ratio to 66 percent in 1971.

Differentials of this order of magnitude appear to have persisted since 1956 (Table 8). Indeed, a slight increase in the differential seems to have occurred from 1956 to 1969. Part of the source of the increasing differential was the relatively low rate of growth in the earnings of female clerical workers and female operatives, who in 1970 accounted for 32 percent and 14 percent, respectively, of all women workers. On the other hand, the rate of growth of earnings of women in the professions was high (a 5.1-percent annual compound rate between 1955 and 1968) relative to all workers; more recently it was even high relative to male professionals.

A large differential is also evident when the comparison is restricted to men and women of the same age and education. As Chart 2 indicates, the incomes of women do not increase with age in anything like the same way men's do. Thus the differential widens with age through much of the working life.

One important factor influencing the differential is experience. The lack of continuity in women's attachment to the labor force means that they will not have accumulated as much experience as men at a given age. The relatively steeper rise of men's income with age has been attributed to their greater accumulation of experience, of "human capital" acquired on the job. Since very few women have participated in the labor force to the same degree as men, it is difficult to set up direct comparisons between the earnings of men and women with the same lifetime pattern

TABLE 8. *Ratio of Total Money Earnings of Civilian Women Workers to Earnings of Civilian Men Workers, Selected Years, 1956–71*

Occupational group	Actual ratios					Adjusted ratios [1]	
	1956	1960	1965	1969	1971	1969	1971
Total [2]	63.3	60.7	59.9	58.9	59.5	65.9	66.1
Professional and technical workers	62.4	61.3	65.2	62.2	66.4	67.9	72.4
Teachers, primary and secondary schools	([3])	75.6	79.9	72.4	82.0	([3])	([3])
Managers, officials, and proprietors	59.1	52.9	53.2	53.1	53.0	57.2	56.8
Clerical workers	71.7	67.6	67.2	65.0	62.4	70.0	66.9
Sales workers	41.8	40.9	40.5	40.2	42.1	45.7	47.4
Craftsmen and foreman	([4])	([4])	56.7	56.7	56.4	60.8	60.2
Operatives	62.1	59.4	56.6	58.7	60.5	65.4	66.6
Service workers excluding private household workers	55.4	57.2	55.4	57.4	58.5	62.5	63.2

1. Adjusted for differences in average full-time hours worked since full-time hours for women are typically less than full-time hours for men.
2. Total includes occupational groups not shown separately.
3. Not available.
4. Base too small to be statistically significant.

of work. Using data from the Labor Department's longitudinal study of women, referred to above, one study was able to compare the earnings of women working different amounts of time throughout their lives with the earnings of men, most of whom are presumed to work continuously after leaving school. The figures for men were taken from census data. The women's lifetime work experience was measured as the percentage of years each had worked since leaving school. However, a work year was crudely defined as one in which the women had worked at least six months. Thus no adjustment could be made for whether the years worked had been truly full-time commitments with respect to both hours worked per week and weeks worked per year.

Among the women 30–44 years old in the survey, the gain from continuous work was apparently very large. If we look only at those women who had worked year-round, full-time in 1966, the median wage and salary income for the group who had worked each year since leaving school was $5,618; for those who had worked less than 50 percent of the years since leaving school (al-

CHART 2. *Annual Income by Age for Male and Female High School and College Graduates*

DOLLARS[1] (ratio scale)

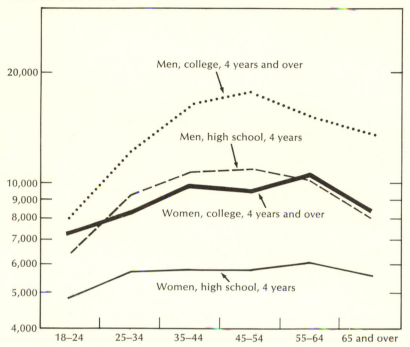

1. Median income of full-time, year-round workers, 1971.

most half the group) the median income was $3,655. The median wage and salary income of men in the same age group who had worked full-time, year-round in 1966 was $7,529. The men are presumed to have worked continuously since leaving school. Thus the women who had worked less than half of the years since leaving school earned only 49 percent as much as men, while the small group of women who had worked each year earned 75 percent as much as men. Interestingly, single women who had worked each year since leaving school earned slightly more than single men. More sophisticated comparisons, adjusting for additional differences in training, continuity at work, and education, can be made. One recent study found that the earnings differential was reduced to below 20 percent after taking account of such differences.

The importance of lifetime accumulated experience in influencing women's earnings suggests one possible explanation for the small decline in the ratio of women's to men's earnings between 1956 and 1969. Since the labor-force participation of women has been rising rapidly, an increasing proportion of new entrants and of those with few accumulated years in the labor force could have resulted in a decline in the average experience level of all women. This drop would in turn temporarily push down the average level of earnings for all women. Unfortunately the data are not available to compare the ratio over a period of time between the earnings of women having a given number of years' experience and the earnings of men.

DIRECT DISCRIMINATION VERSUS ROLE DIFFERENTIATION

A differential, perhaps on the order of 20 percent, between the earnings of men and women remains after adjusting for factors such as education, work experience during the year, and even lifelong work experience. How much of this differential is due to differences in experience or in performance on the job which could not be measured adequately, and how much to discrimination? The question is difficult to answer, in part because there are differences of opinion about what should be classified as discrimination.

Some studies have succeeded in narrowing the male-female differential well below 20 percent. Indeed, Department of Labor surveys have found that the differential almost disappears when men's and women's earnings are compared within detailed job classifications and within the same establishment. In the very narrow sense of equal pay for the same job in the same plant there may be little difference between women and men. However, in this way the focus of the problem is shifted but not eliminated, for then we must explain why women have such a different job structure from men and why they are employed in different types of establishments.

There is clearly prejudice against women engaging in particular activities. Some patients reject women doctors, some clients reject women lawyers, some customers reject automobile saleswomen, and some workers reject women bosses. Employers also may have formulated discriminatory attitudes about women, exaggerating the risk of job instability or client acceptance and therefore excluding women from on-the-job training which would advance their careers.

In fact, even if employers do estimate correctly the average job turnover of women, women who are strongly committed to their jobs may suffer from "statistical discrimination" by being treated as though their own behavior resembled the average. The extent to which this type of discrimination occurs depends on how costly it is for employers to distinguish women who will have a strong job commitment from those who will not. Finally, because some occupations restrict the number of newcomers they take in and because women move in and out of the labor force more often, more women than men tend to fall into the newcomer category and to be thus excluded. For example, restrictive entry policies may have kept women out of the skilled crafts.

On the other hand, as discussed above, some component of the earnings differential and of the occupational differential stems from differences in role orientation which start with differences in education and continue through marriage, where women generally are expected to assume primary responsibility for the home and subordinate their own outside work to their household responsibilities.

It is not now possible to distinguish in a quantitative way between the discrimination which bars women from jobs solely because of their sex, and the role differentiation whereby women, either through choice or necessity, restrict their careers because of the demands of their homes. Some may label the latter as a pervasive societal discrimination which starts in the cradle; nonetheless, it is useful to draw the distinction.

One other missing link in our chain of understanding of these problems is the value of the work done at home by women. One study has found that women college graduates tend to reduce their outside work when their children are small more than less educated women, and that they also devote more time to the training of their children. Of course this pattern is undoubtedly facilitated by the higher income of their husbands. However, this pattern also results in a considerable sacrifice of earnings, and one may infer that these women have therefore placed a very high value on the personal attention they can give their children. Without more information, it is difficult to evaluate the full extent to which women's capabilities have actually been underutilized by society.

The Female-headed Household · In 1971, some 6 million families, about 11.5 percent of all families, were headed by women. These women are widowed, divorced, separated, or single, and many have responsibilities for the support of children in fatherless families or of other relatives. Close to two-thirds of all female-headed families include children; the average number of children under 18 years of age in a female-headed family with children was about 2.3 in 1971, about the same as in male-headed families with children.

As a result of the division of labor within families, the average woman who has been married has not had the same labor-market experience or vocationally oriented training as her husband. Unless she has a substantial alimony or pension, she is likely to face financial difficulties. The median income of female-headed families was $5,116 in 1971, less than half the income of male-headed families ($10,930). When women who head families were full-time, year-round workers, the family's median income was $7,916; but only 32 percent of women heading families were able to be full-time, year-round workers. And the woman who heads a family and works has additional expenses of child care and other home care expenses.

The problems faced by the woman who heads a household are particularly acute if the woman is black, and 27 percent of women heading households are black. For this group, median family income was only $3,645 in 1971. Although, at higher education levels, black women now earn amounts comparable to white women, those black women who head families are at a disadvantage compared to white women. The median personal income of white women heading households and working year-round, full-time was $6,527 in 1971, compared to $5,227 for black women in the same position.

As a result of the combination of a large number of dependents and the difficulty of maintaining the dual responsibility of monetary support and home care, many female-headed families fall below the low-income level. In 1971, 34 percent of female-headed families were below the low-income level, compared to 7 percent for male-headed families. Among black households with a female head, 54 percent were below the low-income level. A large proportion receive public assistance. In 1971, 30 percent of the women heading households received public assistance payments.

It has been suggested, though not proved, that widespread availability of public assistance has encouraged husbands to desert their wives or wives to leave their husbands in families where the husband earns little more than the amount of welfare benefits his family would be entitled to in his absence. Remarriage may also be discouraged because the low-income mother would then lose her entire public stipend, including the child support portion, and without some outside child support a man might be reluctant to marry a woman with several children.

Among the women who are now welfare recipients many are handicapped by lack of education and training and are not in a position to earn an income that would lift them and their families above poverty levels. A program established in 1967, the Work Incentive Program, now gives many mothers currently on welfare, training and placement assistance so that they can improve their ability to support themselves and their dependents.

The Income Tax · Devising a tax system which is equitable and efficient has always posed formidable problems, and often the best solution is one involving compromise with one or more of the objectives. The tax treatment of working wives is one of the more difficult problems. The income tax law as such treats men and women equally and, indeed, its effects on single men and single women are the same. However, some of the features of the tax structure, which have been considered desirable for other purposes, have, as a by-product, unequal effects on the second earner of a married couple, who is usually the wife.

Only income arising from market transactions is taxed. Indeed, there is no practical way to assign a market value to the unpaid work performed at home and then subject it to the tax. As a result, the tax system imposes a general bias in the economy favoring unpaid work at home compared to paid work in the market. However, the bias and the resulting disincentive toward market work are particularly relevant for the married woman who traditionally has done more work at home.

An equity problem also arises from this situation. To use a

hypothetical example, a husband and wife each earning $8,000 would pay the same income tax as a couple where the husband alone works and earns $16,000, although the couple with two earners will have the additional expenses of buying the services which would be produced at home and untaxed if the wife did not work.

There is the further problem that a married couple may pay more or less income tax than two single persons whose combined income equals the couple's, depending upon how the income is divided between the two individuals. This problem reflects a basic ambivalence about whether the appropriate unit of taxation is the individual or the family.

Remedies for the situation are not easy to find. One suggestion has been to allow working wives to deduct a given percentage of their earnings from their income for tax purposes. However, this would be unfair to single persons, who also incur expenses of going to work. A general earned income credit has also been suggested, but this creates a bias against investments in capital and in favor of wage income.

As discussed below, the Revenue Act of 1971 has given expanded tax relief to working wives with children by allowing more liberalized child care deductions to couples within a given income range. This provision, however, does not affect couples without children or couples with combined incomes outside the allowable income range.

Child Care · Provision for child care is a cost to working mothers and a major obstacle to the employment of many other mothers who would work outside the home if they could find satisfactory arrangements for taking care of their children. As more mothers have taken jobs outside the home, and more weigh the possibility of doing so, several major questions about child care have become intense national issues.

One question is whether the government should pay for part or all of the cost of child care. This question is usually raised about the federal government, but it could be equally asked about state or local governments. According to one view of the matter parents have chosen to have children, which implies a certain allocation of their resources, therefore they have no reason to burden other taxpayers to look after the children. Another view of the matter is that government subsidies can be justified and different groups have cited different reasons. The point has been made that the pressures of custom result in a bias against the wife going to work while the husband stays home with the children. A child-care subsidy for working mothers would help remove any harmful effects of this cultural bias. Another reason given is that there is a national interest in the proper care of children, who are, of course, the future nation, and that this case justifies government subsidies. The analogy commonly given is to public education.

Government has given subsidies to families with children but there has been no consistent philosophy behind them. At the extreme, with respect to children in very poor families, we have long recognized the need for public assistance in the form of the program of Aid to Families with Dependent Children. This program is not specifically addressed to children with working mothers. In fact, until recently it was tilted *against* helping working mothers. The federal government also provides a form of assistance for child care through the income tax. With the Revenue Act of 1971, a much more liberal deduction than had ever been provided was instituted specifically for child-care expenses incurred by working wives. Below a combined husband-wife income of $18,000, a working wife can now deduct up to $400 a month for child care expenses. The deduction is scaled downwards to zero as combined income goes from $18,000 to $27,600. The two groups not covered are women whose family income is too low to benefit from a tax deduction and women at the other end of the income scale.

Public discussion of government support for child care has not clearly distinguished among several possible objectives:

(a) To reward and assist the care of all small children;

(b) To assist the care of small children whose parents might not be otherwise able to care for them;

(c) To assist the care of the small children of working mothers;

(d) To assist in the care of small children in a particular way —through day-care institutions, or at home, etc.

Both the amount of government support that is desiarable, and the form it should take if it is to be provided, depend on the choice made among these objectives.

Recently, publicly supported institutional group care, or day care, has received considerable attention as one approach to helping the working mother. Some have also stressed day care as a developmental program. It may be noted that a very small proportion of working women have depended on group day care in an institutional center. A government-sponsored survey of 1965 found that, among employed mothers of children under 6, only 6.4 percent depended on school or group care centers. About 47 percent of the women arranged to have their children cared for at home, often by a relative. The rest mainly arranged for care in someone else's home (31 percent) or looked after the child while working (15 percent).

Some have attributed the low use of day care to a failure of the market to provide a service that would be utilized if financing were available. Others have interpreted it as an indication that the true demand for institutional day care is low. Even among more affluent and knowledgeable working mothers who presumably could afford it, dependence on institutional group care is low. A survey of college graduates found that in 1964, among those who worked and who had children under 6 years, 9 percent used group care, which included nursery schools, kindergartens, and day-care centers. Most (73 percent) arranged for care in their own home.

Whether institutional day care provides the best use of dollars spent on child care has yet to be established. While the issue has not been resolved, it is clear that the problems of mothers who want and need to work require serious attention and a continuing search for new solutions.

GOVERNMENT ACTION

Government has been profoundly concerned with promoting full equality of opportunity for women within both the public and the private sectors. Two approaches have been followed. The first involves the use of law and regulations where they are both applicable and compatible with other goals of a democratic society.

A number of laws have been passed and Executive Orders issued which deal with discrimination by employers. Included are the Equal Pay Act of 1963, requiring employers to compensate men and women in the same establishment equally for work of equivalent skill and responsibility, and Title VII of the Civil Rights Act of 1964, which prohibits discrimination in hiring, discharging, compensation, and other aspects of employment. Title VII is administered by the Equal Employment Opportunity Commission (EEOC). The Equal Employment Opportunity Act, signed by the President in 1972, gave the EEOC enforcement power through the courts in sex-discrimination cases. In December 1971, Order No. 4, under Executive Order 11246, was extended to women. This Order requires federal contractors employing more than 50 workers and holding contracts of $50,000 or more to formulate written affirmative action plans, with goals and timetables, to ensure equal opportunities. Title IX of the Education Amendments of 1972 prohibits discrimination in educational programs or activities on the basis of sex.

The Equal Rights Amendment to the Constitution, which was strongly supported by the President, passed the Senate on March 22, 1972, and has now been ratified by 22 states. The proposed amendment would provide that "equality of rights under the law shall not be denied or abridged by the United States or by any State on account of sex," and would authorize the Congress and the states to enforce the amendment by appropriate legislation. The purpose of the proposed amendment would be to provide constitutional protection against laws and official practices that treat men and women differently.

The other approach of government to providing equality to women has been through leadership. The Women's Bureau in the Department of Labor has for 50 years been concerned with the problems of women at work. Recently, several new groups, each concerned with different areas affecting women, have been formed. The formation of the Advisory Committee on the Economic Role of Women is one such effort. The Citizen's Advisory Council on the Status of Women is another. The latter is a council of private citizens appointed by the President, which surveys the social and political issues of particular interest to women and makes recommendations for legislation or other suitable social action. In an effort to recruit women to top-level jobs in the government, the President in 1971 appointed to the White House staff a special assistant for this purpose. As a result many women have been placed in key policy-making positions, positions never before held by women.

It is only in the past few years that the problems women face as a group have been given the widespread recognition they deserve. There is much to be learned before we can even ask all the appropriate questions. Many of the problems involve profound issues of family and social organization. By listening to diverse groups and to the discussion of the public it is hoped that government will be able to find its appropriate role. . . .

The Economic Role of Women: An Appraisal

BARBARA R. BERGMANN AND IRMA ADELMAN

Professors Barbara Bergmann and Irma Adelman of the University of Maryland discuss their agreements and disagreements with the views of the Council of Economic Advisers expressed in the preceding selection.

THE 1973 Economic Report of the President devotes an entire chapter to the economic role of women in the United States. In this chapter, the Report recognizes that economic discrimination against women exists and, by the length and thoroughness of the analysis describing its dimensions and consequences, implies that such discrimination constitutes a serious economic (and social) problem. The Report does not attempt to minimize the extent to which job segregation, earnings differentials, and higher unemployment rates exist, and the lack of improvement in each component over the last few decades.

As economists, we are particularly pleased to have the official imprimatur of an Economic Report on the view that discrimination does indeed exist. Some economists have the tendency to minimize the importance of nonpecuniary forces in influencing decisions made within the firm, and have been reluctant to admit the possibility of discrimination unrelated to real or perceived productivity differences. We believe that a proper analysis of discrimination is yet to come; such an analysis will have to fuse elements of economics, sociology, psychology, and history. Employers *do* refuse to hire women for certain occupations. Instead they hire men exclusively and pay them more than they would have to pay women of equal ability. The court records are now full of such cases, but such data will never be explained on the basis of a model which includes in the objective function of the employer only monetary profits. Nor can models which assume that employers' decisions about hiring are based on inborn, unchanging, unexplained "tastes" do justice to the social forces, both internal and external to the firm, which bear on such decisions.

Specifically, it is well known that the average woman college graduate who works full time all year ends up with about the same income as the average male high school dropout. The gross earnings differential works out to be between 35 and 57 percent, depending on the data base used to make the calculation. The Report puts the differential due to discrimination at about 20 percent, but this seems low. In a recent article, Isabel Sawhill reviewed seven econometric studies of male-female earnings patterns. In six of them, the differences which could be attributed to discrimination were above 29 percent and ranged up to 43 percent. The seventh study estimated the difference which might be attributable to discrimination as 12 percent, but arrived at this figure by classifying as nondiscriminatory the differences in the distribution of men and women among detailed occupations. Since employers will typically restrict certain jobs to men and since this restriction is a principal mode of discrimination, a major part of the difference in occupational distribution must be classed as due to discrimination. The fact that women in the past have not trained for or applied for such jobs has been due more to women's realism about the prospects for payoff of such training or applications than to women's voluntary embrace of a benign "role differentiation."

The Report places a great deal of emphasis on the fact that women of a given age have up to now averaged less work experience than men of that age. This emphasis on work experience would be justified if experience for women meant the same as experience for men, but, unfortunately, it does not. Women typically are relegated to jobs in which experience adds little to productivity. Consider the newly hired junior executive and his newly hired secretary. They both may have gone to the same college, got the same grades, and even have majored in the same subject. But, for him, experience will mean learning, increased responsibilities, increased contacts, increased self-realization. In her case, it is likely that the development of work skills will have ceased in six months. The Report documents a strong trend towards increase in labor market attachment in women of child-bearing age; this trend will do little good in decreasing the earnings gap unless occupations are desegregated.

The difference in earning power between men and women is an important contributor to the incidence of poverty and welfare dependency in this country. In 1971, 40 percent of families "with female head" were classified as poor as compared to 7 percent of families "with male heads." [1] The wages offered to working women (particularly black women) frequently provide incomes close to or below the amounts welfare mothers get out of welfare.

With respect to job segregation, the Report indicates (on the basis of an analysis of the proportion of women in 197 occupations) that women tend to be concentrated in "women's occupations," and that there has been only a very small change in the direction of less segregation between 1960 and 1970. We have retabulated the 1960 and 1970 census data by occupation given in the Report in a way which shows quite graphically the continued occupational segregation of women (Table 1). In 1960, 73.3 percent of the women workers were in those occupations in which (in 1960) women were grossly overrepresented; in 1970

TABLE 1. *Employment by Sex in Occupations Classified by Extent of Women's Representation in 1960*
(*thousands*)

Occupations in which women were (in 1960)	1960			1970		
	Women	Men	Total	Women	Men	Total
Underrepresented (0–25%)	2,110	31,231	33,341	3,315	32,436	35,751
Well represented (25–45%)	3,503	6,332	9,835	4,470	7,546	12,016
Overrepresented (45–100%)	15,394	5,863	21,257	20,670	6,930	27,600
Total	21,007	43,426	64,433	28,455	46,912	75,367

the proportion was 72.6 percent. The Report's index of occupational segregation, computed somewhat differently, also changed very little. However, this fixity of the degree of segregation meant a deterioration in the position of women, since in 1970 women constituted a greater proportion of the labor force. In 1960, the women in occupations in which women were overrepresented made up 23.9 percent of the labor force. By 1970, the share of women in these occupations in relation to the total labor force had advanced to 27.4 percent. These occupations were already

1. The quotation marks in this sentence convey our disagreement with the Census Bureau's use of the term "head." Census cannot mean by it "highest paid worker" since any family including a husband is classed as being "male headed" regardless of his earnings. They must mean "family boss.

relatively overcrowded in 1960, and as a result, productivity (and wages) were relatively low. This increase in the relative size of these occupations probably increased the amount of overcrowding and further increased the gap between productivity in "men's" and "women's" occupations. This is corroborated by the decrease between 1956 and 1969 in the ratio of female to male earnings (from 63 percent to 59 percent), a large part of which is due to a relative decline in wages of female clerical workers.

The Report documents the fact that women have generally higher unemployment rates than men and that this differential has been more pronounced in recent years. It ties the worsening trend to the relatively large increase in the labor force participation of women. We agree that the increase in labor-force participation rate for women is a part of the cause but not for the reason given in the Report. There emphasis is placed on the fact that a person entering the labor force necessarily has a spell of unemployment while looking for a job. While this is true, the length of such spells and thus the unemployment rate is influenced by the number of job slots for which women are considered eligible as compared with the number of women in the labor force. In our view, the unemployment problem of women has worsened relative to the unemployment problem of men for the same reason wage differentials have increased: because of the segregation of women into "women's" occupations which have become relatively more overcrowded due to the relative increase in the female labor force.

The Report also indicates that quit rates and layoff rates are higher for women than for men. The issue of high turnover among workers is one in which cause and effect are hard to disentangle. The common view is that women have high turnover and enter and leave the labor force more frequently than men because of "their [sic] home responsibilities." In fact, of course, women are consigned for the most part to jobs that have very little interest, opportunity, or pay. Typically, women's jobs are also those for which there is no penalty for high turnover; whether one stays or whether one quits and gets another such job immediately or after an interval, the results in terms of pay and advancement remain much the same. Men who happen to be in this kind of job also have high turnover. Women's relatively high quit rates (2.6 percent per month as opposed to 2.2 percent for men, uncorrected for occupational differences) are seen by some as justifying the exclusion of women from good jobs and by others as an effect of their exclusion. Some may argue that women will have to get over their "lesser attachment to the labor force" before better jobs will open to them, and others may argue that employers will have to open better jobs to women before such improvements in women's turnover can be expected. In fact, these two things will have to occur simultaneously.

The Report gives currency to the recently prominent view that a high turnover rate among women is important in explaining their higher unemployment rates. This view derives, in our opinion, from a misinterpretation of the undoubted fact that all unemployed persons have a history of being separated from a job or entering the labor force. Both turnover *and* the balance of supply and demand for a group's services affect its unemployment rate, but the latter factor is likely to be of far greater importance than the former.

There are, in the Report, a number of instances which we feel reflect a great deal of sociological conservatism. The treatment of paid work outside the home is an example:

Women work outside the home for the same reason as men. The basic reason is to get the income that can be earned by working. Whether —for either men or women—work is done out of necessity or by choice is a question of definition. If working out of necessity means working in order to sustain biologically necessary conditions, probably a small proportion of all the hours of work done in the United States, by men or women, is necessary. If working out of necessity means working in order to obtain a standard of living which is felt by the worker to be desirable, probably almost all of the work done by both men and women is necessary. [p. 116] [2]

This passage, while clearly reflecting liberal intentions, misses some very important reasons why women (and men) work. They work not only to contribute to the family's funding for goods and services, but for greater personal autonomy in spending, for status inside and outside the family, to occupy themselves in an interesting way, to meet people, to have the excitement of being in a contest for advancement, to reduce the amount of housework they do, and to get away from spending all day with their children. The jobs most women now have tend to fulfill these desires

2. [Page references are to material in the Report as reprinted in this volume.—*Editors.*]

to a less satisfactory extent than the jobs men now have, but they frequently fulfill them better than staying home would.

A woman's work also reduces her own financial uncertainty. A working woman whose husband dies or whose marriage breaks up is in a far better economic position than a similarly bereft housewife in terms of experience, entree, contracts, work habits, and asset ownership. In this day of unstable marriages, a woman who refrains from working during marriage is taking a risky position with her own financial future and that of her children. One year after divorce only 38 percent of ex-husbands are in full compliance with court-ordered child support payments. After five years, the figure drops to 19 percent.

One of the reasons given in the Report for women's greater unemployment, turnover, and lower wages is that "a wife seldom is free to migrate to wherever her own prospects are best" [p. 127]. This statement represents prejudicial past practice and is not necessarily the way things will be in the future. Although casual empiricism is our only source of data on this, it seems to us that the practice of considering only the man's career is far less prevalent than it used to be. The economic problem of couples with specialized job requirements is not really going to be an easy one to solve. One possibility for professional people is geographic mobility early in life, with a postponement of marriage until the person has settled into the slot he or she is willing to occupy from then on. A second is lessened mobility throughout life, which could not necessarily be to the detriment of the quality of life in this country. A third is the removal of institutional barriers to joint employment. A fourth is the couple's agreement to move to a location where the partner who is weakest in the labor market has the best chance.

Along a similar vein, the Report assumes that when women have children there is no alternative but to drop out of the labor force for a number of months or years. The present authors themselves are exceptions to this "rule." Speaking of those higher-income women who do drop out, the Report notes "a considerable sacrifice of earnings" and infers "that these women have therefore placed a very high value on the personal attention they can give their children" [p. 137]. Here again we would argue that it is unfruitful to analyze decisions concerning child rearing as being based on unchanging internalized tastes. The appearance of Betty Friedan's book seems to have lowered by quite a lot the "value on the personal attention [women] can give their children." Some women now believe that a lower quantity of personal attention measured in terms of time may increase the quality of that attention to the gain of both children and their parents.

One outstanding omission in the Report is any discussion of changes in the distribution of household tasks between husband and wife, an issue which surely goes to the heart of the women's liberation movement.

The Report asserts there is no practical way to assign a market value to the unpaid work performed at home, subject it to income tax, and thus to tax it comparably with other income and so remove the bias in favor of unpaid work at home. This is quite untrue. The new deduction for paid child care is precisely a move to treat paid and unpaid work similarly. (If domestic work is performed by a family member on an unpaid basis, the value of the service is automatically "deductible," since it is not reported as income.) A deduction for salaries for all paid domestic work by non-family members would seem to be the logical extension. If it is argued that this would favor the rich, then the deduction could be reduced for higher income groups and/or a maximum put on the size of the deduction, and further might be made contingent on all family adults being in the labor force or at school.

In discussing policy with respect to employment discrimination, the Report mentions the many Titles, Acts, and Executive Orders which mandate an end to unfair employment, promotion, and pay practices. It fails to mention that enforcement efforts have been almost nil, despite the fact that very few if any firms, universities, or even government offices are in compliance. What enforcement efforts have been made have raised up loud cries of reverse discrimination.

The present authors are firmly opposed to reverse discrimination and believe it unnecessary and undesirable. Given a fair shake, there is no doubt in our minds that women can make it to full equality with men in the job market. The problem, as we see it, is one of how to implement the transition to "sex-blind" hiring practices, in the presence of prevalent conscious and subconscious discrimination and role casting (on both sides of the "hiring hall"). In this context, there is much to be said for sensibly administered hiring goals of a statistical nature in preference to mere employer statements of good intentions. Naturally, we do not mean a 50-percent ratio across the board. If, for example, women constitute 35 percent of those who by objective criteria qualify for a given rung of an occupation, they should have approximately 35 percent of those jobs, especially in large firms whose very size makes it possible to assume that departures from the average cannot be explained on purely statistical grounds.

To summarize, the chapter of the President's Economic Report on the economic role of women is a creditable coverage of the data, of the problems, and of the issues. It touches almost all the bases one would expect. What would have been welcome and what is missing is a rather more open view of what the problem is, and what the future possibilities are for changing the economic and social role of women. While painting an accurate, reasonably bleak picture of existing reality, the Report tends to underestimate the possibilities and need for social change, and to underemphasize the role of noneconomic forces in having brought about the current situation. Almost absentmindedly, it ignores the transformations in social relations and attitudes and in economic practices which seem to be occurring and which must accelerate if significant change is to occur. Unfortunately also, the Report suggests very little by way of positive programs. . . .

Wage Behavior and the Cost-Inflation Problem

WILLIAM G. BOWEN AND RONALD L. OAXACA

William G. Bowen is President of Princeton University, and Ronald L. Oaxaca teaches at the University of Massachusetts at Amherst.

THE ROLE OF WAGE behavior in the inflationary process has been one of the most hotly debated issues of the postwar years, both in this country and abroad. This is a new development. Prior to the end of World War II most discussions of inflation paid little, if any, attention to wage determination. Inflation was analyzed mainly in terms of changes in the stock of money and in aggregate spending relative to the supply of goods and services. Needless to say, it has long been recognized that increased demand for goods and services leads to increased demand for labor, and that inflationary pressures originating on the demand side have effects on money wages, which in turn affect prices. Recognition of these relationships has led to the adoption of anti-inflationary labor-market policies, especially in wartime, when many governments have instituted wage (and price) controls. In most situations in which wage controls have been employed, however, policy-makers have tended to see an excess of demand over supply as the root problem, and to assume that labor markets play a rather passive, transmission-belt role in the inflationary process.

When World War II ended, the inflationary pressures which accompanied it did not end, although they abated considerably. Economists in many Western European countries and in the United States began to speak of a "new" type of inflation, commonly referred to as "cost inflation." While there are almost as many versions of cost inflation as there are economists who write on the subject, all versions refer, often loosely, to situations in which prices are pushed up from the cost side (cost-push) rather than pulled up from the demand side (demand-pull), and all assign to wage behavior a much more active role than it plays in demand-inflation models.

A SIMPLE COST-INFLATION MODEL

Let us consider the sequence of events in one very simple model of the cost-inflation process. The first component of the model is a wage-determination assertion which states that, in the absence of excess demand for labor, the collective-bargaining process generates wage increases which are greater than increases in productivity. As a result, unit labor costs rise.[1] Next comes a price-determination assertion which states that businessmen price on some kind of cost-plus basis, and that therefore they will respond to increases in unit labor costs by raising product prices. The third, and last, assertion is the monetary-fiscal policy assertion: Those responsible for monetary-fiscal policies will take whatever expansionary steps are necessary to enable consumers to continue to buy roughly the same quantity of goods at the higher prices now being charged.

This simple model has the virtue of calling attention to the interaction between the cost-push and demand-pull aspects of almost any inflationary process. That is, while in the case being

1. At this juncture it may be helpful to some readers if we illustrate the arithmetic of the wage–productivity–unit-labor-cost relationship, since it occupies such an important place both in the model of the cost-inflation process and in the policy debate concerning the famous "guidelines" formulated by the Council of Economic Advisers. To begin with a definition, "unit labor cost" (ULC) is just what its name implies: the dollar cost of the labor needed to produce one unit of output. It can be expressed as $ULC = \frac{W}{P}$, where W is the wage rate per hour and P is "productivity" (output per hour). Thus, if the wage rate were $1.00 and if one man could produce 5 units of output in one hour, unit labor cost would be $\frac{\$1.00}{5} = \$0.20$. It follows from this definitional relationship that if both wages per hour and productivity increase at the same percentage rate, unit labor cost will be unchanged. Suppose, for instance, that both W and P go up 40 percent; then $ULC = \frac{\$1.40}{7} = \$0.20$. The basic point is that increases in wage payments per hour lead to increases in unit labor costs only if productivity increases at a slower rate than wages per hour.

considered here it is a large wage increase which initiates the process (conceptually, it could just as easily be an autonomous increase in profit margins or in the prices of imported raw materials), "appropriate" monetary- or fiscal-policy responses are necessary to prevent the process from being choked off for lack of sufficient demand. Suppose, for instance, that monetary and fiscal policy-makers adopted the policy of not allowing total money spending to rise, no matter what happened. In this situation, a given increase in the price level would require an offsetting reduction in the quantity of goods sold, a derived decrease in the demand for labor, and an increase in unemployment. If wages continued to rise more rapidly than productivity, the cycle would repeat itself and unemployment would increase still more. At what point (if ever) the growing volume of unemployment would dampen wage increases sufficiently to halt the upward pressure on the price level is an empirical question, to which we shall turn shortly.

In the real world, it is of course unlikely that monetary and fiscal policy-makers would be willing to tolerate increasing unemployment. Probably they would ease credit and allow money incomes and money spending to increase sufficiently to permit the same quantity of goods to be purchased as before, thus validating the increase in the price level and setting the stage for another round.

For our present purposes, the important point to note about this cost-inflation model is that it forces monetary and fiscal policy-makers to wrestle with a dilemma: Restrictive policies mean unemployment, but expansionary policies facilitate further rounds of inflation. For this reason, this has been called the "dilemma model" of the inflationary process.

Could things really happen this way? The answer is clearly yes, this kind of cost-inflation model, when carefully stated, is internally consistent. The more difficult—and more interesting—questions, however, are: What kinds of evidence can be used to determine whether in fact we have experienced a significant degree of cost inflation? What does the relevant evidence show? What are the policy implications?

How can we identify cost inflation when we see it? This is not an easy question, and the interaction between cost and demand elements even in the simple model of the cost-inflation process described above makes empirical identification very difficult.

Our main concern here is the wage-behavior aspect of the cost-inflation problem. From this perspective the best measurement approach consists of looking at the relation between unemployment and the rate of change of money wages. This relationship as it has existed in the United States from 1948 to 1970 is depicted in Figure 1.

The first thing to note about this scatter of points is that relatively *low* levels of unemployment have tended to be associated with relatively *large* increases in average hourly earnings. We can obtain a more precise notion of the character of the relationship by fitting a straight line to the scatter of points (RR'). The negative slope of RR' comes as no surprise, since in periods of low unemployment (and tight labor markets), competition by employers for labor leads to larger wage increases than in periods of high unemployment and relatively abundant labor. The bargaining position of a union is of course stronger when unemployment is low and the demand for the employer's product brisk than when the converse conditions hold. Collective bargaining does not operate independently of economic conditions. This simple scatter diagram indicates that it is wrong to suppose that in our economy wages are completely unresponsive to the level of unemployment.

This is certainly not to say, however, that institutional considerations, such as the extent of union organization, employer organization and the basic characteristics of our labor markets, have no influence on wage behavior. In Figure 1, these institutional characteristics can be thought of as influencing the *position* of the RR' curve. If unions were nonexistent, if employers always paid the lowest wage consistent with short-run profit maximization, and if labor were perfectly mobile, then wages would rise less rapidly (and fall more readily) at given levels of unemployment, and the entire RR' sechedule might shift down to, say, II'.

We must also emphasize that, as the dispersion of observations for the individual years around the fitted line testifies, wage behavior is certainly not such a simple phenomenon that all variations in rates of increase can be explained in terms of movements along a stable RR' curve associated with variations in the level of unemployment. Other factors—such as the direction in

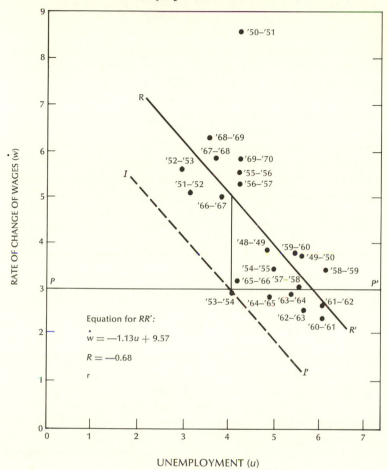

Fig. 1. *The Rate of Change of Money Wages Related to the Level of Unemployment, 1948–1970*

Equation for *RR'*:

$$\dot{w} = -1.13u + 9.57$$

$$R = -0.68$$

RATE OF CHANGE OF WAGES ($\dot{w}$)

UNEMPLOYMENT (u)

The "rate of change of wages" (w) is, more accurately, the percentage rate of change in gross average hourly earnings in manufacturing from one year to the next. "Unemployment" (u) is the average percentage of the civilian labor force unemployed over each two-year span. Thus, $w_{55-56} = \dfrac{w_{56}-w_{55}}{w_{55}}$ and $u_{55-56} = \dfrac{u_{55} + u_{56}}{2}$. The reasons for aligning the wage and unemployment series in this manner are explained at length in W. G. Bowen and R. A. Berry, "Unemployment Conditions and Movements of the Money Wage Level," *Review of Economics and Statistics*, May 1963, pp. 171–172. The data are from the *Manpower Report of the President*, 1971, pp. 219, 264.

If the figures for the Korean War ('50–'51) are omitted, the coefficient of correlation r goes up to $-.79$ and the regression equation becomes $w = -1.05u + 9.00$.

which unemployment is changing, the level of profits, the movement of the consumer price index, overtime provisions, and the timing of key negotiations—also exert influence. Furthermore, as the effect of the outbreak of the Korean War on price and wage increases between 1950 and 1951 illustrates, sudden changes in expectations can have a pronounced short-run effect.

We could speculate further on the significance of this scatter of points for wage determination in the U.S. economy, but it is more important to return to the basic question posed at the beginning of this section: the relevance of wage behavior for the cost-inflation controversy. As noted earlier, cost inflation poses a serious policy problem because it implies that we may experience inflation even during periods of significant unemployment. From the standpoint of the contribution of wage behavior to this problem, we saw earlier that unit labor costs increase only when wages go up more rapidly than productivity. Therefore, to measure the contribution of wage-setting mechanisms to cost inflation, it is necessary to examine the movements of money wages relative to productivity at various levels of unemployment.

To translate this proposition into graphic terms, let us assume, for the sake of simplicity, that productivity increases at the rate of 3 percent per year regardless of the level of unemployment. The horizontal line PP' on Figure 1 reflects this assumption. The vertical distance between RR' and PP' indicates the approximate amount by which unit labor costs have risen at various levels of unemployment. At 4 percent unemployment, for instance, where average hourly earnings have tended to increase at the rate of about 5 percent per year, assuming a 3-percent increase in productivity, there is about a 2-percent increase in unit labor costs, measured roughly by line AB. (Strictly speaking, if our wage index increases from 100 to 105 and our productivity index increases from 100 to 103, unit labor costs increase not by 2 percent but by $105/103 = 1.94$ percent.) Figure 1 also suggests that, on the average, it has taken an unemployment rate of slightly less than 6 percent to prevent labor costs from rising at all. So, unless we are prepared to regard 6-percent unemployment as "full employment," we must conclude that, from the wage-setting side, our economy has been subject to "cost inflation," in the sense that unit labor costs have tended to rise before full employment has been reached.

How much of a downward shift in the *RR'* curve would be required to eliminate the policy dilemma altogether depends on how one defines "full employment." If we accept the conservative goal of 4 percent unemployment, then *RR'* would need to pass through point A (as *II'* does), and the extent to which our present situation departs from this "ideal" can be measured in terms of the (average) distance between *II'* and *RR'*. A simpler index can be obtained by calculating the area of triangle *ABC*. This can be done in terms of objective data (we don't need to make assumptions about the exact slope of *II'*). The area of this triangle is intuitively meaningful, in that it is the sum of the *increases* in unit labor costs associated with all levels of unemployment above the "full"-employment level.

Thinking about cost inflation in these terms also provides us with a way of comparing our postwar experience with earlier experiences. In principle, we could fit a line like *RR'* to the observations for earlier years and then compare these results (and the area of the triangle analogous to *ABC*) with the postwar results. Unfortunately, however, the economic history of the United States during much of the first half of the twentieth century was so replete with "unusual" events that many observations have to be discarded. The experience of the 1930s for instance, is strictly *sui generis,* as is the experience with wage controls during World War II. The figures for the first two decades of the 1900s (excluding the World War I years) are less subject to extreme abnormalities, and a comparison of this period with the postwar years does yield several interesting findings. First of all, even in the early 1900s, before the advent of large industrial unions, average hourly earnings tended to increase faster than productivity when the unemployment rate was below 6 percent. So, the limited evidence that is available indicates that cost inflation, viewed from the wage side, is by no means a distinctly new phenomenon. The data also suggest, however, that at comparable rates of unemployment average hourly earnings in manufacturing tended to rise more rapidly in the postwar years than in the period prior to 1930. Postwar wage behavior does seem to be somewhat less conducive to the simultaneous achievement of price stability and high-level employment than wage behavior in the early part of the century.

POLICY IMPLICATIONS

In this country, main reliance has been placed on aggregate demand measures (monetary and fiscal policies) in our efforts to achieve a reasonable degree of price stability and relatively high employment. In terms of Figure 1, these tools can be thought of as moving us along a given wage-unemployment-reaction curve (approximated by RR') to whatever point seems most desirable from the standpoint of society's preferences for low unemployment versus price stability.[2]

The menu of choices given by the position of the RR' curve is such that, over a considerable range, the makers of monetary and fiscal policies must expect to face both an unemployment problem and some upward pressure from the cost side on the price level. Furthermore, the slope of RR' implies that taking steps to ease one problem will aggravate the other problem. In short, the policy dilemma suggested by the simple cost-inflation model is real enough.[3]

It would be wrong to infer that monetary and fiscal policies cannot be used to halt "cost inflation." A sufficient reduction in aggregate demand would presumably move us down the RR' line to point C, where unit labor costs are stable. But the important point is that by taking such action, we would allow substantial unemployment to develop at the same time. Many people have commented on the relative stability of labor costs and

2. Actually, the specific mix of monetary and fiscal policies used in a given situation will also have some influence on the shape and position of RR'. For instance, if we were to increase aggregate demand by means of a substantial increase in public expenditures for space exploration, we would be much more likely to encounter bottlenecks at relatively high levels of overall unemployment than if the same increase in aggregate demand were brought about by a widely diffused tax cut. Thus, if the increased space-expenditure route were taken, the increase in aggregate demand would probably lead to a somewhat larger increase in wages (because of the shortage of space workers) and a somewhat smaller increase in employment than if the tax-cut route had been taken. In terms of Figure 1, RR' would be farther to the right and somewhat steeper in the space-expenditure case than in the tax-cut case.

3. To be more precise, the evidence presented here indicates that the dilemma is a real one provided that the upward pressure on prices exerted by increases in production-worker labor costs in manufacturing is not offset by decreases in other labor costs, in nonlabor costs, in profit margins, or in the prices of imported goods. Conceptually, these other elements could, of course, worsen as well as improve the menu of policy choices.

prices in the U.S. in the past, but they sometimes fail to note that relative stability has been accompanied by considerable unemployment.

This policy dilemma cannot be solved by wishing it away, or by saying that to admit that there can be a conflict of goals is to display a "lack of faith in America." Given the present nature of our labor and product markets, the makers of monetary and fiscal policies must face up to the need for making hard-headed choices. How bad is a 1-percent increase in the price level vis-à-vis having an additional 1 to 1½ percent of the labor force unemployed?

In addition to trying to find the optimal point on the present RR' line, policy-makers may also try to shift the entire line to a more advantageous position. Proposals to reduce the market power of unions and corporations and to return to a more atomistic type of economy may have this as one objective. It is well to remember, however, that the link between union size and union power may be weak and, moreover, that the relationship between union power and the size of wage settlements may be more complex than it at first appears to be. In fact, some scholars have suggested that we move in the other direction, that we emulate some foreign countries by encouraging more centralization of bargaining so that the national interest will loom larger in the thinking of the negotiators. In evaluating proposals for institutional reform, it is very important to remember that participation in wage-setting is only one of the functions of unions (probably not the most important), and that a proposal designed to weaken a union's bargaining power in the wage arena may also weaken its ability to protect its members from arbitrary treatment.

Union-busting and trust-busting are certainly not the only possible ways of seeking to shift RR' down to a lower level. Wage controls can also be used, and have been in wartime, though they raise serious problems of administration, allocation, and equity. The exhortations of public officials and the publication of "guideposts" for wage- and price-setting constitute a less extreme, though nonetheless controversial, approach to the problem, as other articles in this volume indicate. As noted earlier, shortages of workers in particular areas or with particular skills can also put upward pressure on labor costs (by creating "bottlenecks"), and in this connection mention should be made of the increasing efforts in this country to retrain workers and promote mobility.

The purpose of this essay has not been to advocate one policy or another but to clarify the issues and present some relevant evidence as to the trade-offs which exist at the present time. In conclusion, however, we do wish to express the following personal judgments. (1) The cost-inflation problem, while real, has been exaggerated, and it is not serious enough to justify radical institutional surgery. (2) Efforts to increase the adaptability of the labor force are all to the good and will help somewhat to make high employment and price stability more compatible. (3) Carefully directed exhortations of public officials are not likely to do much harm and may even do some good. (4) Finally, what is most important at the present time is an attitude of realism and a willingness to accept somewhat greater risks of inflation than we accepted in the 1957–1963 period in order to reduce what we regard as an intolerably high level of unemployment.

Noninflationary Wage and Price Behavior

COUNCIL OF ECONOMIC ADVISERS

The Council of Economic Advisers was established to advise the President by the Employment Act of 1946. Of all the words published since then by various Councils, none has been so widely quoted and discussed as this statement from the January 1962 Economic Report of the President.

THERE ARE IMPORTANT segments of the economy where firms are large or employees well-organized, or both. In these sectors, private parties may exercise considerable discretion over the terms of wage bargains and price decisions. Thus, at least in the short run, there is considerable room for the exercise of private power and a parallel need for the assumption of private responsibility.

Individual wage and price decisions assume national importance when they involve large numbers of workers and large amounts of output directly, or when they are regarded by large segments of the economy as setting a pattern. Because such decisions affect the progress of the whole economy, there is legitimate reason for public interest in their content and consequences. An informed public, aware of the significance of major wage bargains and price decisions, and equipped to judge for itself their compatibility with the national interest, can help to create an atmosphere in which the parties to such decisions will exercise their powers responsibly.

How is the public to judge whether a particular wage-price decision is in the national interest? No simple test exists, and it is not possible to set out systematically all of the many considerations which bear on such a judgment. However, since the question is of prime importance to the strength and progress of the American economy, it deserves widespread public discussion and clarification of the issues. What follows is intended as a contribution to such a discussion.

Mandatory controls in peacetime over the outcomes of wage negotiations and over individual price decisions are neither desirable in the American tradition nor practical in a diffuse and decentralized continental economy. Free collective bargaining is the vehicle for the achievement of contractual agreements on wages, fringes, and working conditions, as well as on the "web of rules" by which a large segment of industry governs the performance of work and the distribution of rewards. Similarly, final price decisions lie—and should continue to lie—in the hands of individual firms. It is, however, both desirable and practical that discretionary decisions on wages and prices recognize the national interest in the results. The guideposts suggested here as aids to public understanding are not concerned primarily with the relation of employers and employees to each other, but rather with their joint relation to the rest of the economy.

WAGES, PRICES, AND PRODUCTIVITY

If all prices remain stable, all hourly labor costs may increase as fast as economy-wide productivity without, for that reason alone, changing the relative share of labor and nonlabor incomes in total output. At the same time, each kind of income increases steadily in absolute amount. If hourly labor costs increase at a slower rate than productivity, the share of nonlabor incomes will grow or prices will fall, or both. Conversely, if hourly labor costs increase more rapidly than productivity, the share of labor incomes in the total product will increase or prices will rise, or both. It is this relationship among long-run economy-wide productivity, wages, and prices which makes the rate of productivity change an important benchmark for noninflationary wage and price behavior.

Productivity is a *guide* rather than a *rule* for appraising wage and price behavior for several reasons. First, there are a number of problems involved in measuring productivity change, and a number of alternative measures are available. Second, there is nothing immutable in fact or in justice about the distribution of the total product between labor and nonlabor incomes. Third, the pattern of wages and prices among industries is and should be responsive to forces other than changes in productivity.

Annual Rates of Growth of Output per Man-hour, 1909 to 1960
(based on establishment series)

Industry series	Average annual percentage change [*]			
	1909 to 1960	1947 to 1960	1947 to 1954	1954 to 1960
Total private economy	2.4	3.0	3.5	2.6
Nonagriculture	2.1	2.4	2.7	2.2
Nonmanufacturing	[b]	2.2	2.6	1.9
Manufacturing	[b]	2.8	2.9	2.9
Manufacturing corrected for varying rates of capacity utilization	[b]	2.8	2.8	3.1

[*] Computed from least squares trend of the logarithms of the output per man-hour indexes.
[b] Not available.

SOURCES: Department of Labor and Council of Economic Advisers.

ALTERNATIVE MEASURES OF PRODUCTIVITY

If the rate of growth of productivity over time is to serve as a useful benchmark for wage and price behavior, there must be some meeting of minds about the appropriate methods of measuring the trend rate of increase in productivity, both for industry as a whole and for individual industries. This is a large and complex subject and there is much still to be learned. The most that can be done at present is to give some indication of orders of magnitude, and of the range within which most plausible measures are likely to fall (see table above).

There are a number of conceptual problems in connection with productivity measurement which can give rise to differences in estimates of its rate of growth. Three important conceptual problems are the following:

1. Over what time interval should productivity trends be measured? Very short intervals may give excessive weight to business-cycle movements in productivity, which are not the relevant standards for wage behavior. Very long intervals may hide significant breaks in trends; indeed in the United States— and in other countries as well—productivity appears to have risen more rapidly since the end of the Second World War than before. It would be wholly inappropriate for wage behavior in the 1960s to be governed by events long in the past. On the other hand, productivity in the total private economy appears to have advanced less rapidly in the second half of the postwar

period than in the first.

2. Even for periods of intermediate length, it is desirable to segregate the trend movements in productivity from those that reflect business-cycle forces. Where the basic statistical materials are available, this problem can be handled by an analytical separation of trend effects and the effects of changes in the rate of capacity utilization.

3. Even apart from such difficulties, there often exist alternative statistical measures of output and labor input. The alternatives may differ conceptually or may simply be derived from different statistical sources. A difficult problem of choice may emerge, unless the alternative measures happen to give similar results.

Selected measures of the rate of growth of productivity in different sectors of the economy for different time periods are shown in the table. Several measures are given because none of the single figures is clearly superior for all purposes.

THE SHARE OF LABOR INCOME

The proportions in which labor and nonlabor incomes share the product of industry have not been immutable throughout American history, nor can they be expected to stand forever where they are today. It is desirable that labor and management should bargain explicitly about the distribution of the income of particular firms or industries. It is, however, undesirable that they should bargain implicitly about the general price level. Excessive wage settlements which are paid for through price increases in major industries put direct pressure on the general price level and produce spillover and imitative effects throughout the economy. Such settlements may fail to redistribute income within the industry involved; rather they redistribute income between that industry and other segments of the economy through the mechanism of inflation.

PRICES AND WAGES IN INDIVIDUAL INDUSTRIES

What are the guideposts which may be used in judging whether a particular price or wage decision may be inflationary? The desired objective is a stable price level, within which particular prices rise, fall, or remain stable in response to economic pressures. Hence, price stability within any particular industry is not necessarily a correct guide to price and wage decisions in that industry. It is possible, however, to describe in broad outline a set of guides which, if followed, would preserve over-all price stability while still allowing sufficient flexibility to accommodate objectives of efficiency and equity. These are not arbitrary guides. They describe—briefly and no doubt incompletely—how prices and wage rates would behave in a smoothly functioning competitive economy operating near full employment. Nor do they constitute a mechanical formula for determining whether a particular price or wage decision is inflationary. They will serve their purpose if they suggest to the interested public a useful way of approaching the appraisal of such a decision.

If, as a point of departure, we assume no change in the relative shares of labor and nonlabor incomes in a particular industry, then a general guide may be advanced for noninflationary wage behavior, and another for noninflationary price behavior. Both guides, as will be seen, are only first approximations.

The general guide for noninflationary wage behavior is that the rate of increase in wage rates (including fringe benefits) in each industry be equal to the trend rate of over-all productivity increase. General acceptance of this guide would maintain stability of labor cost per unit of output for the economy as a whole —though not of course for individual industries.

The general guide for noninflationary price behavior calls for price reduction if the industry's rate of productivity increase exceeds the overall rate—for this would mean declining unit labor costs; it calls for an appropriate increase in price if the opposite relationship prevails; and it calls for stable prices if the two rates of productivity increase are equal.

These are advanced as general guideposts. To reconcile them with objectives of equity and efficiency, specific modifications must be made to adapt them to the circumstances of particular industries. If all of these modifications are made, each in the specific circumstances to which it applies, they are consistent with stability of the general price level. Public judgments about the effects on the price level of particular wage or price decisions should take into account the modifications as well as the general guides. The most important modifications are the following:

1. Wage rate increases would exceed the general guide rate in an industry which would otherwise be unable to attract sufficient labor; or in which wage rates are exceptionally low compared with the range of wages earned elsewhere by similar labor, because the bargaining position of workers has been weak in particular local labor markets.

2. Wage rate increases would fall short of the general guide rate in an industry which could not provide jobs for its entire labor force even in times of generally full employment; or in which wage rates are exceptionally high compared with the range of wages earned elsewhere by similar labor, because the bargaining position of workers has been especially strong.

3. Prices would rise more rapidly, or fall more slowly, than indicated by the general guide rate in an industry in which the level of profits was insufficient to attract the capital required to finance a needed expansion in capacity; or in which costs other than labor costs had risen.

4. Prices would rise more slowly, or fall more rapidly, than indicated by the general guide in an industry in which the relation of productive capacity to full employment demand shows the desirability of an outflow of capital from the industry; or in which costs other than labor costs have fallen; or in which excessive market power has resulted in rates of profit substantially higher than those earned elsewhere on investments of comparable risk.

It is a measure of the difficulty of the problem that even these complex guideposts leave out of account several important considerations. Although output per man-hour rises mainly in response to improvements in the quantity and quality of capital goods with which employees are equipped, employees are often able to improve their performance by means within their own control. It is obviously in the public interest that incentives be preserved which would reward employees for such efforts.

Also, in connection with the use of measures of over-all productivity gain as benchmarks for wage increases, it must be borne in mind that average hourly labor costs often change through the process of up- or down-grading, shifts between wage and salaried employment, and other forces. Such changes may either add to or subtract from the increment which is available for wage increases under the over-all productivity guide.

Finally, it must be reiterated that collective bargaining within an industry over the division of the proceeds between labor and nonlabor income is not necessarily disruptive of over-all price stability. The relative shares can change within the bounds of noninflationary price behavior. But when a disagreement between management and labor is resolved by passing the bill to the rest of the economy, the bill is paid in depreciated currency to the ultimate advantage of no one.

It is no accident that productivity is the central guidepost for wage settlements. Ultimately, it is rising output per man hour which must yield the ingredients of a rising standard of living. Growth in productivity makes it possible for real wages and real profits to rise side by side.

Rising productivity is the foundation of the country's leadership of the free world, enabling it to earn in world competition the means to discharge its commitments overseas. Rapid advance of productivity is the key to stability of the price level as money incomes rise, to fundamental improvement in the balance of international payments, and to growth in the nation's capacity to meet the challenges of the 1960s at home and abroad. That is why policy to accelerate economic growth stresses investments in science and technology, plant and equipment, education and training—the basic sources of future gains in productivity.

What Price Guideposts?

MILTON FRIEDMAN

This and the following essay are a widely discussed exchange on the desirability of wage and price controls or guideposts. Although written in the context of the controversy surrounding the Kennedy Administration's guidepost policy, the arguments are a nearly perfect reflection of the debate that surrounded the Nixon Administration's "new economic policy" adopted in the fall of 1971 and that surround the issue of expanding the powers of the Council on Wage and Price Stability, formed in 1974.

THE STUDENT OF INFLATION is tempted to rejoin, "I've heard that one before," to exhortations now emanating from Washington. Since the time of Diocletian, and very probably long before, the sovereign has repeatedly responded to generally rising prices in precisely the same way: by berating the "profiteers," calling on private persons to show social responsibility by holding down the prices at which they sell their products or their services, and trying, through legal prohibitions or other devices, to prevent individual prices from rising. The result of such measures has always been the same: complete failure. Inflation has been stopped when and only when the quantity of money has been kept from rising too fast, and that cure has been effective whether or not the other measures were taken.

The first section of this paper explains why the attempts to hold down individual wages and prices have failed to stop inflation. Direct control of prices and wages does not eliminate inflationary pressure. It simply shifts the pressure elsewhere and suppresses some of its manifestations.

Inflation is always and everywhere a monetary phenomenon, resulting from and accompanied by a rise in the quantity of money relative to output. This generalization is not an arithmetical proposition or a truism, and it does not require a rigid relation between the rates of rise in prices and in the quantity of money. The precise rate at which prices rise for a given rate of rise in the quantity of money depends on such factors as past price behavior, current changes in the structure of labor and product markets, and fiscal policy. The monetary character of inflation, as the second section points out, is an empirical generalization backed by a wide range of evidence which suggests that substantial changes in the demand for money seldom occur except as a reaction to a sequence of events set in train by changes in the quantity of money. It follows that the only effective way to stop inflation is to restrain the rate of growth of the quantity of money.

Given inflationary pressure, rises in recorded or quoted prices and wages can be suppressed to some extent. The less severe the inflationary pressure, and the more vigorous and effective the enforcement of price controls, the greater the extent to which the manifestations of inflation can be suppressed. As the third section points out, such suppressed inflation is far more harmful, both to efficiency and freedom, than open inflation, and the more effective the suppression, the greater the harm. It is highly desirable to avoid inflation but if, for whatever reason, that is not feasible, it is far better that inflation be open than that it be suppressed.

The final section of the paper asks what harm, if any, will be done by the guideposts. Even granted that compulsory price and wage controls cannot stop inflation and can do great harm, may not some measure of voluntary compliance by businessmen and union leaders ease the tasks of other instruments of policy and enable businessmen and union leaders to display their sense of social responsibility? In my opinion, the answer is clearly in the negative. Compliance with the guideposts is harmful because it encourages delay in taking effective measures to stem inflation, distorts production and distribution, and encourages restrictions on personal freedom.

Entirely aside from their strictly economic efforts, guidelines threaten the consensus of shared values that is the moral basis of a free society. Compliance with them is urged in the name of social responsibility; yet, those who comply hurt both themselves and the community. Morally questionable behavior—the evading of requests from the highest officials, let alone the violation of legally imposed price and wage controls—is both privately and socially beneficial. That way lies disrespect for the law on the part of the public and pressure to use extralegal powers on the part of officials. The price of guideposts is far too high for the return, which, at most, is the appearance of doing something about a real problem.

I. WHY DIRECT CONTROL OF PRICES AND WAGES DOES NOT ELIMINATE INFLATIONARY PRESSURE

An analogy is often drawn between direct control of wages and prices as a reaction to inflation and the breaking of a thermometer as a reaction to, say, an overheated room. This analogy has an element of validity. Prices are partly like thermometers in that they register heat but do not produce it; in both cases, preventing a measuring instrument from recording what is occurring does not prevent the occurrence. But the analogy is also misleading. Breaking the thermometer need have no further effect on the phenomenon being recorded; it simply adds to our ignorance. Controlling prices, insofar as it is successful, has very important effects. Prices are not only measuring instruments, they also play a vital role in the economic process itself.

A much closer analogy is a steam-heating furnace running full blast. Controlling the heat in one room by closing the radiators in that room simply makes other rooms still more overheated. Closing all radiators lets the pressure build up in the boiler and increases the danger that it will explode. Closing or opening individual radiators is a good way to adjust the relative amount of heat in different rooms; it is not a good way to correct for overfueling the furnace. Similarly, changes in individual prices are a good way to adjust to changes in the supply or demand of individual products; preventing individual prices from rising is not a good way to correct for a general tendency of prices to rise.

Suppose that there is such a general tendency, and suppose that some specific price (or set of prices), say, the price of steel, is prevented from rising. Holding down the price of steel does not make more steel available; on the contrary, given that other prices and costs are rising, it reduces the amount that producers can afford to spend in producing steel and is therefore likely to reduce the amount available from current production. Holding down the price of steel does not discourage buyers; on the contrary, it encourages consumption. If the suppressed price is effectively enforced and not evaded by any of the many channels that are available to ingenious sellers and buyers some potential buyers of steel must be frustrated—there is a rationing problem. Chance, favoritism, or bribery will have to decide which buyers succeed in getting the steel. Those who succeed pay less than they are willing to pay. They, instead of the steel producers, have the remainder to spend elsewhere. Those who fail will try to substitute other metals or products and so will divert their demand eleswhere; the excess pressure is shifted, not eliminated.

The situation is precisely the same on the labor market. If wages are tending to rise, suppressing a specific wage rise will mean that fewer workers are available for that type of employment and more are demanded. Again rationing is necessary. The workers employed have less income to spend, but this is just balanced by their employers having larger incomes. And the unsatisfied excess demand for labor is diverted to other workers.

But, it will be said, I have begged the question by *starting* with a general tendency for prices to rise. Can it not be that this general tendency is itself produced by rises in a limited number of prices and wages which in turn produce sympathetic rises in other prices and wages? In such a case, may not preventing the initial price and wage rises nip a wage-price or price-price spiral in the bud?

Despite its popularity, this cost-push theory of inflation has very limited applicability. Unless the cost-push produces a monetary expansion that would otherwise not have occurred, its effect will be limited to at most a temporary general price rise, accompanied by unemployment, and followed by a tendency toward declining prices elsewhere.

Suppose, for example, a strong (or stronger) cartel were formed in steel, and that it decided to raise the price well above the level that otherwise would have prevailed. The price rise would reduce the amount of steel people want to buy. Potential purchasers of steel would shift to substitute products, and no doubt the prices of such substitutes would tend to rise in sympathy. But there is now another effect. Steel producers would hire fewer workers and other resources. These would seek employment elsewhere, tending to drive down wages and prices in other industries. True, wages and prices might be sticky and decline only slowly, but that would only delay the downward adjustments and only at the expense of unemployment.

A textbook example is provided by John L. Lewis and the

United Mine Workers. Coal mining hourly earnings rose by "163 percent from 1945 to 1960. Bituminous coal mining employment dropped from 284,000 to 168,000. By way of comparison, in the same period, manufacturing production hourly earnings rose . . . 122 percent and manufacturing employment rose." High coal prices undoubtedly put upward pressure on the prices of oil and gas; but the high unemployment put downward pressure on other prices.

The only example I know of in United States history when such a cost-push was important even temporarily for any substantial part of the economy was from 1933 to 1937, when the NIRA, AAA, Wagner Labor Act, and associated growth of union strength unquestionably led to *increasing* market power of both industry and labor and thereby produced upward pressure on a wide range of wages and prices. This cost-push did not account for the concomitant rapid growth in nominal income at the average rate of 14 percent a year from 1933 to 1937. That reflected rather a rise in the quantity of money at the rate of 11 percent a year. And the wage and cost-push had nothing to do with the rapid rise in the quantity of money. That reflected rather the flood of gold, initiated by the change in the United States price of gold in 1933 and 1934 and sustained by the reaction to Hilter's assumption of power in Germany.

The cost-push does explain why so large a part of the growth in nominal income was absorbed by prices. Despite unprecedented levels of unemployed resources, wholesale prices rose nearly 50 percent from 1933 to 1937, and the cost of living rose by 13 percent. Similarly, the wage cost-push helps to explain why unemployment was still so high in 1937, when monetary restriction was followed by another severe contraction.

The popularity of the cost-push theory of inflation, despite its limited applicability, stems I believe from two sources: first, the deceptiveness of appearances; second, the desire of governmental authorities to shift the blame for inflation.

One of the fascinating features of economic relations is the frequent contrast between what is true for the individual and what is true for the community. Time and again the one is precisely the opposite of the other. Each individual takes for granted the prices of the things he buys and regards himself as having no effect on them; yet, consumers as a whole greatly affect those prices by the combined effects of their separate actions. Each individual can determine the amount of currency he carries around in his pocket; yet, all individuals together may have nothing to say about the total amount of currency to be carried around; that may be determined by monetary authorities, the individuals being free only to shuffle it around and transfer it from one to the other. Indeed, it is precisely this contrast between what is true for the individual and for the community that underlies many, perhaps most, common economic fallacies. They arise from invalid generalization from the individual to the community.

The widespread belief in the cost-push theory of inflation is a striking example. To each businessman separately, inflation tends to come in the form of increasing costs, and, typically, he correctly regards himself as having to raise the price at which he sells because his costs have risen. Yet, those cost rises may themselves reflect an increase in demand elsewhere and simply be part of the process whereby the demand increase is transmitted; and his ability to raise his price without a drastic decline in sales reflects the existence of excess demand. The monetary expansion and the associated increase in money demand take place through mysterious, widely dispersed, and largely invisible channels. The cost and price increases are their visible tracks.

In a recent elementary economics textbook, Alchian and Allen have given a vivid illustration of how a price rise produced by a demand increase can make itself felt to almost all the participants in the process as a cost-push:

Pretend that for some reason people's desire for meat increases. . . . Housewives reveal an increased demand by buying more meat than formerly at the current prices in the meat markets. . . . [T]he increased demand takes its toll of inventories. . . . [T]he butcher will buy more meat than usual the next day in order to restore his inventory from its abnormally low level. . . . Just as butchers use inventories, so packers . . . also rely on inventories. . . . [A]ssume that the first day's change in demand was within that inventory limit and therefore was met without a price increase.

Packers restore inventories by instructing their cattle buyers . . . to buy more cattle than usual. But with all the packers restoring their inventories in this manner, the number of cattle available for sale each day are inadequate to meet the increased total demand *at the old price*. . . .

[T]he buyers will begin to raise their offers . . . until the price

rises to the point where the packers will not want to buy more meat
. . . than is available from the cattlemen. . . .

[T]he packers experience *a rise in costs* . . . [so] the packers must
charge a higher price to butchers if they are to continue as profitable
meat packers. . . . The butchers, in turn, post higher prices to the
housewives. When housewives complain about the higher price, the
butcher in all innocence, honesty, and correctness says that it isn't
his fault. The cost of meat has gone up. . . . And the packers can
honestly say the same thing.

To almost all participants, therefore, a rise in price produced
by excess demand appears to take the form of a rise in costs that
enforces a higher price.

The interpretation of inflation as a reflection of cost-push is
greatly fostered by governmental authorities. In modern times,
the government has direct responsibility for the creation and
destruction of money; it determines what happens to the quantity
of money. Since inflation results from unduly rapid monetary expansion, the government is responsible for any inflation that
occurs. Yet, governmental authorities, like the rest of us, while
only too eager to take credit for the good things that occur, are
most reluctant to take the blame for the bad things—and inflation generally is regarded as a bad thing. Their natural tendency
is to blame others for the inflation that governmental policies
produce—to castigate the rapacious businessman and power-
hungry labor leader rather than point to the government printing
press as the culprit.

The 1966 *Annual Report* of the Council of Economic Advisers
is an amusing and distressing example. It has a 31-page chapter
on "Prospects for Cost-Price Stability" that so far as I have been
able to determine has only two passing references to "monetary
policy" and does not even contain the word "money"—a treatment of money strictly comparable to the way a rigid Puritan
writing a book about love might have handled "sex." In the page
and a half section on "Determination of the Price Level," there is
no mention of the government's role until the last of eight para-
graphs where the main emphasis is on the government's role as
a customer and on governmental measures that directly affect
costs. The one sentence in this section on the government's role
in affecting aggregate demand is simply: "Fiscal policies help
determine the overall size of markets" (p. 65). Similarly, in the

Council's explicit discussion of monetary policy elsewhere in the report (pp. 44–52), there is no reference at all to inflation or price level, although there is a passing reference to "spending." The careful reader of this 186-page report will have to wait until page 176, in a historical chapter on experience under the Employment Act, to find the first explicit recognition that there is any relation between monetary policy and inflation!

II. INFLATION IS A MONETARY PHENOMENON

Yet, the central fact is that inflation is always and everywhere a monetary phenomenon. Historically, substantial changes in prices have always occurred together with substantial changes in the quantity of money relative to output. I know of no exception to this generalization, no occasion in the United States or elsewhere when prices have risen substantially without a substantial rise in the quantity of money relative to output or when the quantity of money has risen substantially relative to output without a substantial rise in prices. And there are numerous confirming examples. Indeed, I doubt that there is any other empirical generalization in economics for which there is as much organized evidence covering so wide a range of space and time.

Some confirming examples are extremely dramatic and illustrate vividly how important the quantity of money is by comparison with everything else. After the Russian Revolution of 1917, there was a hyperinflation in Russia when a new currency was introduced and printed in large quantities. Ultimately, it became almost valueless. All the time, some currency was circulating which had been issued by the prerevolutionary Czarist government. The Czarist government was out of power. Nobody expected it to return to power. Yet, the value of the Czarist currency remained roughly constant in terms of goods and rose sharply in terms of the Bolshevik currency. Why? Because there was nobody to print any more of it. It was fixed in quantity and therefore it retained its value. Another story has to do with the United States Civil War. Toward the end of the war, the Union troops overran the place where the Confederates had been printing paper money to finance the war. In the course of moving to a new location, there was a temporary cessation of the printing of money. As a result, there was also a temporary interruption in the price rise that had been proceeding merrily.

The fact that inflation results from changes in the quantity of money relative to output does not mean that there is a precise, rigid, mechanical relationship between the quantity of money and prices, which is why the weasel-word "substantial" was sprinkled in my initial statement of the proposition. First, over short periods, the rate of change in the quantity of money can differ and sometimes by appreciable amounts from the rate of change in nominal income or prices because of other factors, including fiscal policy. Second, and more important, changes in the quantity of money do not make their effects felt immediately. It may be six months or a year and a half before a change in the quantity of money apreciably affects nominal income or prices. Failure to allow for this difference in timing is a major reason for the misinterpretation of monetary experience. Third, and most important of all, there is a systematic and regular difference between changes in money and in prices in the course of an inflationary episode that is itself part of the very process by which monetary changes produce changes in prices.

The typical life history of an inflation is that the quantity of money per unit of output initially increases more rapidly than prices. During this period, the public does not anticipate price rises, interprets any price rise that occurs as temporary, and hence is willing to hold money balances of increased "real" value (i.e., corresponding to a larger volume of goods and services) in the belief that prices will be lower in the future. If the quantity of money continues to increase faster than output, however, prices will continue to rise, and sooner or later the public will come to anticipate further price rises. It then wishes to reduce its money balances not only to their former real value but to an even smaller level. Cash has now become a costly way to hold assets, since its purchasing power is decreasing. People therefore try to reduce their cash balances. They cannot, as a whole, do so in nominal terms (i.e., in terms of dollars), because someone or other must hold the amount in existence. But the *attempt* to do so bids up prices, wages, and nominal incomes. The result is to reduce "real" balances. During this stage, therefore, prices rise more rapidly than the quantity of money, and sometimes much more rapidly. If the rate of rise of the quantity of money stabilizes, no matter at how high a level, the rate of price rise will ultimately settle down also. The total price rise may bear very different relations to the rise in the quantity of money per unit of output depending on the size of the monetary expansion. In moderate inflations, as for example the rise in prices in the United States by a third from 1896 to 1913, prices and money may rise by about the same percentage. In really substantial inflations, such as have occurred in recent decades in many South American countries, the price rise will generally be several times the monetary rise; in hyperinflations, the price rise will be many times the monetary rise.

The United States today is in the early stages of such an episode. From 1961 to 1965, the quantity of money per unit of output rose more rapidly than prices—the typical initial reaction. From early 1965 to early this year [1966], the monetary rise has been accelerated, and the price rise has accelerated even more rapidly as anticipations of inflation have become widespread. As of now, if the rate of monetary growth were stabilized at the high level attained in 1965, the rate of price rise would continue to accelerate for a time. Even if the rate of monetary growth were sharply reduced, prices would continue to rise for a time under the combined influence of earlier monetary growth and changing anticipations.

Why should money be so critical a factor in price level behavior? Why should it occupy such a central role in the process? The key to an answer is the difference, already referred to, between the *nominal* quantity of money, the quantity of money expressed in terms of dollars, and the *real* quantity of money, the quantity of money expressed in terms of the goods and services it will buy or the number of weeks of income it is equal to.

People seem to be extraordinarily stubborn about the real amount of money that they want to hold and are unwilling to hold a different amount, unless there is a strong incentive to do so. This is true over both time and space.

Let me illustrate with currency in circulation alone, which is more comparable among countries and over time than a broader definition of money, including deposits. In the United States, the amount of currency held by the nonbanking public amounts to roughly four weeks' income. I know that this result seems surprising. When I ask people separately whether they have as much as four weeks' income in the form of currency, I have rarely had anyone say yes. Part of the explanation is that about one-fifth of the currency is held by businesses such as retail stores. The main explanation, I am sure, is that there are a small number of people who hold very large sums in this form while the rest of us hold more moderate amounts. In any event, that is what the figures show. The fascinating thing is that the corresponding number was not very different a century ago. In 1867 people on the average held about five weeks' income in the form of currency, compared to today's four weeks' income. In the interim this number has gone as low as 2¼ weeks' income in 1929, as high as 8½ weeks' in 1946. That is a substantial range, it is true, but those are long periods spanning major changes in circumstance.

This range, moreover, contains the figures for most countries in the world. In Israel, the amount held is about the same as in the United States, a little over four weeks' income; in Japan and Turkey, about five weeks' income; in Greece and Yugoslavia, about six weeks' income; in India, about seven weeks' income. Again, these are not negligible differences; yet, they are small compared to the differences among the countries in wealth, economic structure, political forms, and cultural characteristics.

Even these relatively small differences over time and space can be largely explained by a few major factors, of which the prevalence of deposit banking is perhaps the single most important.

Given that people are so stubborn about the amount they hold in the form of money, let us suppose that, for whatever reasons, the amount of money in a community is higher than people want to hold at the level of prices then prevailing. It does not for our purposes matter why, whether because the government has printed money to finance expenditures or because somebody has discovered a new gold mine or because banks have discovered how to create deposits. For whatever reason, people find that although on the average they would like to hold, let us say, the four weeks' income that they hold in the United States, they are actually holding, say, five weeks' income. What will happen? Here again it is essential to distinguish between the individual and the community. Each individual separately thinks he can get rid of his money and he is right. He can go out and spend it and thereby reduce his cash balances. But for the community as a whole the belief that cash balances can be reduced is an optical illusion. The only way I can reduce my cash balances in nominal terms is to induce somebody else to increase his. One man's expenditures are another man's receipts. People as a whole cannot spend more than they as a whole receive. In consequence, if everybody in the community tries to reduce the nominal amount of his cash balances, on the average nobody will do so. The amount of nominal balances is fixed by the nominal quantity of money in existence and no game of musical chairs can change it.

But people can and will try to reduce their cash balances and the process of trying has important effects. In the process of trying to spend more than they are receiving, people bid up the prices of all sorts of goods and services. Nominal incomes rise and real cash balances are indeed reduced, even though nominal balances, the number of dollars, are not affected. The rise in prices and incomes will bring cash balances from five weeks' income to four weeks' income. People will succeed in achieving their objective, but by raising prices and incomes rather than by reducing nominal balances. In the process, prices will have risen by about a fifth. This in a nutshell and somewhat oversimplified is the process whereby changes in the stock of money exert their influence on the price level. It is oversimplified because there is a tendency to overshoot, followed by successive readjustments converging on the final position, but this complication does not affect the essence of the adjustment process.

Emphasis on the key role of the quantity of money leaves open the question of what produced the changes in the quantity of money. Hence, if an analysis of inflation is to deal not only with the change in the quantity of money but with what brought it about, it will be a very pluralistic theory. Historically, the actual sources of monetary expansion have been very different at different times and in different places.

In United States history, the most dramatic inflations have been wartime inflations—those associated with the Revolution, when prices skyrocketed and the declining value of the money produced the phrase "not worth a continental," and with the War of 1812, the Civil War, and the two world wars, in all of which prices roughly doubled. In these episodes, the increase in the quantity of money was produced mainly by the printing of money to pay for governmental wartime expenses.

But even these episodes are not wholly to be explained in that fashion. In the final year of the World War I inflation (1919–20), when prices rose at their most rapid pace, the government budget was in surplus, and the rapid increase in the quantity of money was being produced for private, not governmental, purposes.

The two main periods of peacetime inflation in the United States were in the 1850s and from 1896 to 1913. Both were parts of worldwide movements. The first resulted from the gold discoveries in California, the second from the development of a commercially feasible cyanide process for extracting gold from low-grade ore plus gold discoveries.

There is a widespread belief that inflation is somehow related to government deficits. This belief has a sound basis. The existence of deficits tempts governments to finance them by printing money (or the equivalent, creating deposits), hence deficits have often been the source of monetary expansion. But deficits per se are not necessarily a source of inflation. As already noted, the federal budget ran a surplus during 1919–20 when prices rose rapidly; similarly, there were extremely large surpluses immediately after World War II, when prices also rose rapidly. On the other side, the budget was in deficit during 1931–33, when prices fell sharply. Deficits can contribute to inflation by raising interest rates and so velocity; for the rest they are a source of inflation if and only if they are financed by printing money.

The same considerations apply to other alleged sources of inflation. Increasingly strong trade unions can be a source of inflation if by their actions they produce unemployment and if a government committed to full employment expands the quantity of money as part of a policy of eliminating unemployment. This particular chain of events has often been alleged but, as already noted, seldom observed in the United States. More generally, a full employment policy can be a source of inflation if it produces undue monetary expansion.

III. SUPPRESSED INFLATION IS WORSE THAN OPEN INFLATION

The distinction between inflation and deflation, important as it is, is less important than the distinction between open inflation, one in which prices are free to rise without governmental price controls, and suppressed inflation, one in which the government attempts to suppress the manifestations of the inflationary pressure by controlling prices, including prices not only of products but also of factor services (i.e., wage rates, rents, interest rates) and of foreign currencies (i.e., exchange rates).

Open inflation is harmful. It generally produces undesirable transfers of income and wealth, weakens the social fabric, and may distort the pattern of output. But if moderate, and especially if steady, it tends to become anticipated and its worst effects on the distribution of income are offset. It still does harm, but, *so long as prices are free to move,* the extremely flexible private enterprise system will adapt to it, take it in stride, and continue to operate efficiently. The main dangers from open inflation are twofold: first, the temptation to step up the rate of inflation as the economy adapts itself; second, and even more serious, the temptation to attempt cures, especially suppression, that are worse than the disease.

Suppressed inflation is a very different thing. Even a moderate inflation, if effectively suppressed over a wide range, can do untold damage to the economic system, require widespread government intervention into the details of economic activity, destroy a free enterprise system, and along with it, political freedom. The reason is that suppression prevents the price system from working. The government is driven to try to provide a substitute that is extremely inefficient. The usual outcome, pending a complete monetary reform, is an uneasy compromise between official tolerance of evasion of price controls and a collectivist economy. The greater the ingenuity of private individuals in evading the price controls and the greater the tolerance of officials in blinking at such evasions, the less the harm is done; the more law-abiding the citizens, and the more rigid and effective the governmental enforcement machinery, the greater the harm.

A dramatic illustration of the difference between open and suppressed inflation is the contrast between the experience of Germany after World War I and after World War II. This happens to be one of those beautiful examples that history turns up for us from time to time in which experience is almost in the nature of a controlled experiment, because the difference in the character of the monetary phenomena is so great compared to differences in other relevant respects. After World War I, Germany had an open inflation of extremely large magnitude. It is difficult for us to contemplate the kind of inflation Germany experienced at that time because it is so extreme. A student of mine, Phillip Cagan, wrote a doctoral dissertation on hyperinflation in different countries, which has become something of a classic. He had the problem of how to define hyperinflation. He defined it as beginning when prices started to rise at the rate of more than 50 percent a month. In the German hyperinflation after World War I, there were periods when prices rose not 50 percent a month but doubled every week and some occasions on which they were doubling every day. Indeed, it got to the point that firms started to pay their employees their wages three times a day—after breakfast, lunch, and dinner, so that they could go out and spend them before they lost their value. That was really a whopping inflation, yet it went on for something like three years.

The inflation did untold harm to Germany. The impoverishment of the middle classes, the arbitrary redistribution of income, and the frantic instability unquestionably helped to lay the groundwork for Hitler's emergence later. Looked at, however, from the purely technical point of view of its effect on production, the astounding thing is that until the last six months of the inflation, total output in Germany never declined. Indeed, Germany never declined. Indeed, Germany was one of the few countries in the world that did not experience a great depression in 1920–21, when prices in the gold standard part of the world dropped by 50 percent. Total output remained up. Why? Because the inflation was open. Prices were allowed to rise freely and hence the price system could still be used to allocate resources. Of course, after a time people started to use all sorts of escalation devices to link their contracts to the value of the mark in the foreign exchange market, which was also a free market price, and so on. The price system, however, could work even under those handicaps.

After World War II, Germany was under inflationary pressure as a result of an increase in the quantity of money during the war and the fixation of prices. By our usual standards, the pressure was substantial. If prices had been allowed to rise freely immediately after the war, the price level would probably have quadrupled. That is a large price rise. But it is negligible by comparison with the price rise after World War I which has to be described in terms of factors like 10^{10}. The price rise after World War II, however, was suppressed. Ordinarily, it is extremely difficult to suppress a price rise of that magnitude, to enforce price control when the market price would be four times the controlled price. But there were certain especially favorable circumstances from the point of view of enforcing price control in Germany at that time. Germany was occupied by the armed forces of Britain, France, and the United States, and the occupation forces enforced price control.

The result of suppressing inflation was that output in Germany was cut in half. The price system was not allowed to function. People were forced to revert to barter. Walter Eucken in an article describing this period tells the story of people who worked in a factory making pots and pans. They would work there for two or three days and then they would be given their pay in the form of aluminum saucepans. They would take the saucepans and spend the rest of the week scouring the countryside trying to find some farmer who would be willing to trade a few potatoes or other produce for the saucepans. That is not a very efficient way to organize resources. It was so inefficient that something had to be done and something was done. People developed their own forms of money. Cigarettes came into use as money for small transactions and cognac for large transactions—the most liquid money I have ever come across. But even with these expedients, suppressed inflation cut output in half from the level at the immediate end of the war.

In 1948 as you know, the so-called German miracle began. It was not a very complicated thing. It amounted to introducing a monetary reform, eliminating price control, and allowing the price system to function. The extraordinary rise in German output in the few years following this reform was not owing to any miracle of German ingenuity or ability or anything like that. It was the simple, natural result of allowing the most efficient technique people have ever found for organizing resources to work instead of preventing it from working by trying to fix prices here, there, and everywhere.

Although this is the most dramatic example, numerous other examples can be cited of a less extreme kind. In the immediate postwar period, I visited Europe and spent some time in Britain and France. Both countries at that time had widespread price controls. But there was an important difference. The people of Britain were relatively law-abiding, the people of France were not. The result was that Braitain was being strangled by the law obedience of her people and France was being saved by the black market.

The reason suppressed inflation is so disastrous, as these examples suggest, is that the price system is the only technique that has so far been discovered or invented for efficiently allocating resources. If that is prevented from operating, something else must be substituted. What do we substitute? It is always some kind of clumsy physical control.

A striking current example is provided by India with its system of exchange control and import licenses. In the past decade, India has experienced a price rise of something between 25 and 50 percent. In the main, this price rise has been open, although there have been some price controls. There has been, however, an important glaring exception—the price of foreign exchange. The official price of the dollar or the pound sterling in terms of the rupee is precisely the same today as it was ten years ago. If the price of the rupee was anywhere close to being right then, it cannot be right now. And of course it is not right. The effect has been to encourage people to try to import goods because they are artificially cheap and to discourage them from trying to export goods because the amount of rupees they can get for the foreign exchange proceeds of exports will buy less at home than before. Imports and exports are highly sensitive areas. Even moderate changes can have very large effects. The result has been a serious foreign exchange crisis. India at first allowed her foreign exchange reserves to run down until today reserves are very small. In addition, direct controls over imports have been increasingly tightened and all sorts of special measures have been taken to subsidize and encourage exports. Certain categories of imports have been banned entirely. For other categories, import licenses have been given on a more and more limited scale. And even so, the exchange rate has been able to be maintained only because of very large additional grants of foreign aid.

The result has been incredible waste and inefficiency, proliferating bureaucracy, and widespread corruption and bribery. In my opinion, the pegging of the exchange rate is the key to

India's economic failure. Setting it free, along with the wiping away of the mountains of regulations exchange control has engendered, is the most important single step that India could take to unleash its very real potentialities.

The experience of India could be duplicated manyfold. I cite it only because it happens to be the case with which I am most intimately familiar. . . .

The United States had widespread experience with the results of price and wage controls during World War II, and New York City's housing difficulties are a current reminder of their long-reaching effects, since New York is the only city in the land that still has rent controls as a heritage of the war. The memory of this experience leads government officials to disavow any intention of imposing explicit price and wage controls. But voluntary controls are no improvement, except as they are more readily evaded. Let them be abided by, and the consequences will be the same.

IV. WHAT HARM WILL BE DONE BY THE GUIDEPOSTS?

Even granted that legally imposed and vigorously enforced wage and price ceilings covering a wide range of the economy would do enormous harm, some may argue that the enunciation of guideposts, their approval by businessmen and labor leaders, and voluntary compliance with them, or even lip service to them, is a palliative that can do no harm and can temporarily help until more effective measures are taken. At the very least, it may be said, it will enable businessmen and labor leaders to display their sense of social responsibility.

This view seems to me mistaken. The guideposts do harm even when only lip service is paid to them, and the more extensive the compliance, the greater the harm.

In the first place, the guideposts confuse the issue and make correct policy less likely. If there is inflation or inflationary pressure, the governmental monetary (or, some would say, fiscal) authorities are responsible. It is they who must take corrective measures if the inflation is to be stopped. Naturally, the authorities want to shift the blame, so they castigate the rapacious businessman and the selfish labor leader. By approving guidelines, the businessman and the labor leader implicitly whitewash the government for its role and plead guilty to the charge. They thereby encourage the government to postpone taking the corrective measures that alone can succeed.

In the second place, whatever measure of actual compliance there is introduces just that much distortion into the allocation of resources and the distribution of output. To whatever extent the price system is displaced, some other system of organizing resources and rationing output must be adopted. As in the example of the controls on foreign loans by banks, one adverse effect is to foster private collusive arrangements, so that a measure undertaken to keep prices down leads to government support and encouragement of private monopolistic arrangements.

In the third place, "voluntary" controls invite the use of extralegal powers to produce compliance. And, in the modern world, such powers are ample. There is hardly a business concern that could not have great costs imposed on it by antitrust investigations, tax inquiries, government boycott, or rigid enforcement of any of a myriad of laws, or on the other side of the ledger, that can see no potential benefits from government orders, guarantees of loans, or similar measures. Which of us as an individual could not be, at the very least, seriously inconvenienced by investigation of his income tax returns, no matter how faithfully and carefully prepared, or by the enforcement to the letter of laws we may not even know about? This threat casts a shadow well beyond any particular instance. In a dissenting opinion in a recent court case involving a "stand-in" in a public library, Justice Black wrote, "It should be remembered that if one group can take over libraries for one cause, other groups will assert the right to do it for causes which, while wholly legal, may not be so appealing to this court." Precisely the same point applies here. If legal powers granted for other purposes can today be used for the "good" purpose of holding down prices, tomorrow they can be used for other purposes that will seem equally "good" to the men in power—such as simply keeping themselves in power. It is notable how sharp has been the decline in the number of businessmen willing to be quoted by name when they make adverse comments on government.

In the fourth place, compliance with voluntary controls imposes a severe conflict of responsibilities on businessmen and labor leaders. The corporate official is an agent of his stockholders; the labor leader, of the members of his union. He has a responsibility to promote their interests. He is now told that he must sacrifice their interests to some supposedly higher social responsibility. Even supposing that he can know what "social responsibility" demands—say by simply accepting on that question the gospel according to the Council of Economic Advisers—to what extent is it proper for him to do so? If he is to become a civil servant in fact, will he long remain an employee of the stockholders or an agent of the workers in name? Will they not discharge him? Or, alternatively, will not the government exert authority over him in name as in fact?

V. CONCLUSION

Inflation being always and everywhere a monetary phenomenon, the responsibility for controlling it is governmental. Legally enforced price and wage ceilings do not eliminate inflationary pressure. At most they suppress it. And suppressed inflation is vastly more harmful than open inflation.

Guideposts and pleas for vluntary compliance are a halfway house whose only merit is that they can more readily be abandoned than legally imposed controls. They are not an alternative to other effective measures to stem inflation, but at most a smokescreen to conceal the lack of action. Even if not complied with they do harm, and the more faithfully they are complied with, the more harm they do. . . .

The Case Against the Case Against
the Guideposts

ROBERT M. SOLOW

Robert Solow, professor of economics at the Massachusetts Institute of Technology, responds to Friedman's attack on guidepost policies.

I CHOOSE THIS defensive-sounding title because it points to an important truth. The wage-price guideposts, to the extent that they can be said to constitute a policy, are not the sort of policy you would invent if you were inventing policies from scratch. They are the type of policy you back into as you search for ways to protect an imperfect economy from the worst consequences of its imperfect behavior. For this reason, it seems to me that the best way to start an evaluation of the wage-price guideposts is with recognition of the dilemma to which they are a response.

THE PROBLEM OF PREMATURE INFLATION:
SOME OBVIOUS REMEDIES

The problem is that modern mixed capitalist economies tend to generate unacceptably fast increases in money wages and prices while there is not general excess demand. No particular view of the economic process or of the determinants of demand need be implied by this observation. It is a fact, however, or at least it is widely believed to be a fact, that wages and prices begin to rise too rapidly for comfort while there is still quite a bit of unemployed labor and idle productive capacity and no important bottlenecks. This tendency creates a dilemma for public policy. Governments generally do not wish to acquiesce in an inflationary spiral; indeed, in our rather international trading world, governments may not be able to do so. On the other hand, governments value employment and output, for the very good reason that people value employment and output, so governments generally do not wish to choke off economic expansion while there is room for more.

This dilemma is not confined to the United States. Most of the advanced capitalist economies of the world have faced it, despite the differences in their wage- and price-making institutions. So far as I know, none of them has found a very satisfactory solution; and most of them have been driven to some form of "incomes policy," to something very like the wage-price guideposts. These policies have not been entirely successful either, but that may be too much to expect anyway.

It is no accident that the Council of Economic Advisers launched the local version of incomes policy in the January 1962 Economic Report, despite the fact that the unemployment rate was then near 6 percent and manufacturing capacity only 83 percent utilized, according to the McGraw-Hill survey. Wholesale prices were not then rising, nor did they begin to rise until 1965. But still the Council felt—with good reason—that it had to protect its flank against those who argued, even then, that an expansionary fiscal and monetary policy would dissipate itself almost immediately in inflationary wage and price behavior. The argument proved wrong; but that it could be seriously made suggests the nature and the seriousness of the problem of premature inflation.

Given the character of the problem, it is natural for an economist to turn elsewhere before he settles for anything so weak, so uncertain, and so uneven in its effects as exhortation. In particular, two possible policy lines present themselves as straightforward and natural. The first is simply to accept the universe: The appropriate remedy is either to restrict demand enough through fiscal and monetary means to keep the price level reasonably stable, or else to accept some inflation. The second approach is to recognize that the threat of premature inflation reflects significant departures from perfect competition in labor and product markets: The appropriate remedy is to create or restore competition by breaking up all concentrations of market power, whether in the hands of trade unions or large firms, and by eliminating all or most legal protections against domestic and foreign competition.

Both these suggestions have attractive aspects. The first promises that economic policy can be more or less confined to the im-

personal tools of the fiscal and monetary policy that we know
something about. The second caters to the economist's prejudice
in favor of the mechanism of the competitive market. If there is
a case against the case against the guideposts, part of it has to be
that the first obvious remedy may be very costly, and the second
obvious remedy is more than a little unrealistic.

The experience of the years 1958–64 certainly indicates that
the economy can be run with quite a lot of slack, but not a cata-
strophic amount, so that the price level will more or less police
itself. That is a possible policy. But it is not a costless policy. In
the first place, one of the necessary concomitants of this policy is
a pretty substantial unemployment rate. Since the incidence of
unemployment is typically uneven, and the unevenness has no
claim to equity, common decency requires that this policy be
accompanied by a major reform and improvement of the unemployment compensation system, and possibly of other transfer
payment systems as well. This is a budgetary cost, but not a real
burden on the economy as a whole. In the second place, however, the maintenance of slack does represent a real burden to
the economy as a whole in the form of unproduced output. It
is not easy to make any estimate of that cost. The usual rule of
thumb is that one-half point on the unemployment rate corre-
sponds to something between 1 and 2 percent of real GNP. In
that case, the amount of relief from inflation that could be had
by keeping the unemployment rate one-half point higher than
otherwise desirable would have an annual cost of about $10
billion at 1965 prices and GNP. Just because that is a large
number does not mean that the price is not worth paying.
Everyone must choose for himself. But it does mean that an
alternative policy capable of having the same restraining effect
as a half point of unemployment is a preferable policy unless it
imposes social costs of about that order of magnitude.

The policy of heading off premature inflation by strengthening competition is in many ways the opposite of costly. Most
economists, at least, have a preference for competition, free
trade, mobility, and the like, on the ground that they promote
economic efficiency, while any inequities that may result can
be offset by other means. Most economists, therefore, would
argue in favor of strengthening competition, free trade, and
mobility even if there were no problem of premature inflation;

all the more so, since there might be beneficial effects on the inflation front as well. But realism suggests that significant steps in this direction will be very slow in coming, if they come at all. In the meanwhile, the problem of premature inflation remains, and the unattainable best should not be allowed to become the enemy of the second best. To anyone who argues against guide-posts that competition is the best policy, I reply: Yes indeed, and go to it, but meanwhile, . . .

The logic of a guidepost policy is, I suppose, something like this. In our imperfect world, there are important areas where market power is sufficiently concentrated that price and wage decisions are made with a significant amount of discretion. When times are reasonably good, that discretion may be exercised in ways that contribute to premature inflation. (Institutions with market power may actually succeed in exploiting the rest of the economy temporarily or permanently, or they may see their decisions canceled out almost immediately by induced increases in other prices and wages.) People and institutions with market power may, in our culture, be fairly sensitive to public opinion. To the extent that they are, an educated and mobilized public opinion may exert some restraining pressure to forestall or limit premature inflation.

The January 1962 guideposts were intended to be a step in the educational process. Whatever else they have accomplished, or not accomplished, I think they, and the discussion they aroused, have surely made a dent on public thinking about wage and price behavior. I give an example: In 1962 it was often said that if money wages rose at the same rate as productivity and the price level were constant, labor would in effect appropriate all of the gains in productivity. There may still be people who don't realize that the effect would actually be to increase aggregate wages and aggregate profits at the same rate, preserving their proportional relations to one another. But there must be many fewer such people now.

The object of the guideposts was and is to hold up to the public—and to those participants in wage and price decisions who can exercise some discretion—a summary picture of how wages and prices *would* behave in a fairly smoothly functioning competitive market economy subject neither to major excess demand nor major deficiency of demand. The hope was that active discussion of the issues might induce the participants, in effect, to imitate a little more closely a few aspects of competitive price and wage behavior. If that happened, the expansion of real demand and the production of real output might be able to go a little further before unacceptable increases in the general price level would begin.

I think it is fair to say that no one connected with the guide-posts expects or ever expected that they could have any major role to play either under conditions of generalized excess demand or under conditions of substantial slack in the economy. When unemployment is heavy and excess capacity is widespread, wages and prices are likely to police themselves. To expect the price level as a whole to fall is probably too much, but it is unlikely to rise, and if it does, not very much. Similarly, when demand is excessive in broad sectors of the economy, it is idle to believe that the price level can be talked out of rising. The guidepost idea does rest on the presumption that somewhere in between here is a zone of economic conditions, neither too tight nor too slack, in which there is some tendency toward inflation, but a weak enough tendency so that an informed and mobilized public opinion can have effect.

HAVE THE GUIDEPOSTS HAD AN EFFECT ON WAGES AND PRICES?

The most common criticism of dependence on wage-price guideposts is that they simply do not work and have no effect on either wages or prices. Some of these criticisms simply cancel one another: For every employer who complains that unions take the guidepost figure for a floor, there is a union leader who complains that employers take it for a ceiling. Such evidence is worth nothing. Better evidence can be had, but is in the nature of the case uncertain. We may not be able to tell whether the guideposts have had any influence on wage and price decisions: first because there is no way to measure the "intensity" with which the guideposts have been pressed; and second because we have no universally accepted quantitative doctrine about how prices and money wages are determined in the absence of guideposts.

The best such quantitative explanation I know is that of Professor George Perry of the University of Minnesota. He reconstructs the percentage change in hourly wages in manufacturing from one quarter to the same quarter of the next year in terms of four determinants. The determinants are the unemployment rate, the accompanying change in the Consumer Price Index, the rate of profit on capital in manufacturing, and the change in the rate of profit. He finds, as you would expect, that wages in manunfacturing will rise more rapidly the lower the unemployment rate; the faster the cost of living has been rising, the higher are profits, and the faster they have been rising. The precise relationship is based on the experience of the manufacturing sector from 1948 to 1960; it explains the course of money wages quite well during that period.

When Perry's relationship is used to explain wage changes in manufacturing after 1960, it tells an interesting story. In 1961 and the first half of 1962, wages rose faster than the theory would expect. Beginning with the third quarter of 1962, and without exception for the next fourteen quarters to the end of 1965, wages rose more slowly than the theory would expect. Runs in the residuals are not uncommon, but this run is uncommonly long. Moreover, although the overestimation of wage changes was initially small, it became substantial in 1964 and 1965. In 1965, the annual increase in wage rates was about 1.7 percent lower than the 1948–60 experience would lead one to expect.

Is all of this difference attributable to the influence of the guideposts? Is any? I don't suppose any definite answer can be given. The timing certainly suggests that the guideposts had something to do with it. But econometric inference is rarely completely solid, and I have no doubt that someone who wanted strongly to resist that conclusion could produce a statistical model giving different results.

What does seem fairly clear is that manufacturing wages increased relatively slowly during the middle 1960s, given the unemployment rate actually ruling, the good profits actually earned, and the increase in consumer prices that actually occurred. It is not farfetched to believe that the guideposts might have been an important factor in this structural change.

The object of the guideposts is to stall off premature inflation. Wages themselves are a matter of concern only because they bulk so large in total costs. If the guideposts served only to damp the increase in wages without holding down the price level, then their main result would simply be a transfer of income from wages to profits, and that is not their purpose. So the question arises whether there has been any visible change in price behavior.

All of the obstacles to clear-cut measurement of the wage effects apply equally to the price effects. Moreover, I know of no basic study like Perry's to serve as a starting-point for price behavior. I can report, however, on one small-scale and partial experiment.

Year-to-year changes in the wholesale price index for all manufactures, between 1954 and 1965, can be explained moderately well in terms of the McGraw-Hill index of capacity utilization, and the accompanying year-to-year changes in labor costs per unit of output in manufacturing. As one would expect, the price index rises faster the higher the utilization of capacity and the faster unit labor costs increase. If one amends the relation among these variables to allow for a structural shift after 1962, the data suggest that wholesale prices rose about $7/_{10}$ of a point a year more slowly after 1962 than before, for any given utilization rate and change in unit labor costs. (This suggestion just fails of statistical significance, but I suspect that lengthening the period and refining the data would correct that.)

Although this is the most tentative sort of conclusion, it is double-barreled. Even if there were no structural change in price behavior after 1962, it would mean that any reduction or slowdown in unit labor costs achieved through the guideposts was being passed on into prices to the usual extent. If in fact there was a structural change, it means that over and above the effect through labor costs there was a further tendency for prices to rise more slowly than earlier experience would suggest.

There is, as I have said, no firm reason to attribute these shifts in behavior to the guideposts. Nor is there any reason not to.

WOULD THE GUIDEPOSTS FREEZE THE DISTRIBUTION OF INCOME AND INTERFERE WITH FREE MARKETS?

It is often remarked—as indeed I remarked earlier—that if wage rates on the average were to rise precisely as fast as productivity, while the price levels were to remain constant, then the proportions of the national income going to labor and to property would stay unchanged. To take some very round numbers, suppose production per man-year were $10,000 and the annual wage $7,500, so that $2,500 went to owners of capital. If productivity and the annual wage were both to rise by that famous 3.2 percent, and prices were unchanged, then output per man-year would go to $10,320 and the wage $7,740. This would leave $2,580 in property income. Notice that the $320 of new output per man-year has been divided in the same 75–25 proportions as the original $10,000, so that the overall proportional distribution of the national income is undisturbed.

This algebraic fact has led to criticism of the guidepost concept. The argument is not at all about the equity or justice of the current distribution of income. The argument is that the distribution of income—before taxes and transfers—is part of the market process in our economy. Changes in incomes are supposed to guide efficiently the allocation of resources. To freeze the distribution of income in a pattern that may be suitable to current conditions can lead to distortions and inefficiencies if economic conditions change and call for a changed distribution of income.

It seems to me that this argument has no practical weight at all. It is rendered trivial by two facts. The first is that the division of the national income between labor and property incomes is among the slower-changing characteristics of our economy, or of any Western economy. The second is that neither the guideposts nor any other such quantitative prescription can be satisfied *exactly*. Suppose that wage rates do follow the guideposts exactly. Then if the price level, instead of remaining constant, goes up by, say, 1 percent in a year, the share of wages in national income will fall by 1 percent—that is, by about ¾ of one percentage point. If, on the other hand, the price level should fall by 1 percent, the share of wages in national income would rise by ¾ of 1 percentage point. That may not seem like much, but actually it is quite a lot, more than enough to provide all the flexibility that our economic system is likely to need.

In the twenty years since the end of the war, the proportion of "compensation of employees" to national income has moved about within a narrow range, say from 65 percent to 71 percent. There is no reason to suppose that market forces will always want to keep the figure within those bounds, but there is every reason to believe that market forces will never, or hardly ever, want to move the proportional distribution of income very rapidly. As the numerical example shows, if wages adhered to the guidelines, the distribution of income could get from one end of its postwar range to the other in about eight years, with an annual rate of inflation or deflation never exceeding 1 percent.

There is no practical question, then, of freezing the distribution of income. The normal amount of play in any such policy gives all the room needed for the market to operate. It would be possible to provide formally for more flexibility if that were needed. If the wages guideposts were expressed in terms of a fairly narrow range, say from 3.0 to 3.5 percent per year, this would serve two purposes. For one thing, it would more nearly express the uncertainty in any estimate of the trend increase in productivity. And secondly, it would permit the outcome to be nearer the bottom or the top of the range, depending on "market forces." Even a steady price level would then permit some drift in the distribution of income.

Even apart from this question of distribution, one hears it said that the guideposts are a dangerous interference in the free market, even a form of price control. At least this criticism is inconsistent with the other one that claims the guideposts to be ineffective. With some ingenuity, one could probably cook up a set of assumptions under which the guideposts had no effect on wage-price behavior, yet managed to do harm to the market economy. But this seems farfetched to me. If they are a real interference with the market, they must be partially effective.

I would contend that it is also farfetched to describe the wage-price guideposts as anything remotely like a system of wage and price controls. But in any case I am not concerned with the way the guideposts have been used by this President or that President, but with the way they were intended. They were intended, as I mentioned earlier, as a device for the education and mobilization of public opinion. The January 1962 Economic Report said:

Individual wage and price decisions assume national importance when they involve large numbers of workers and large amounts of output directly, or when they are regarded by large segments of the economy as setting a pattern. Because such decisions affect the progress of the whole economy, there is legitimate reason for public interest in their content and consequences. An informed public, aware of the significance of major wage bargains and price decisions, and equipped to judge for itself their compatibility with the national interest, can help to create an atmosphere in which the parties to such decisions will exercise their powers responsibly. . . . The guideposts suggested here as aids to public understanding are not concerned primarily with the relation of employers and employees to each other, but rather with their joint relation to the rest of the economy. (Pp. 185–86.)

It is no doubt inevitable that an activist President will want to help public opinion along. But that is still a far cry from wage and price control.

Moreover, by both intent and necessity, the guideposts can influence only those wage and price decisions in which the parties have a certain amount of discretion. Atomistic textbook competitors, having no discretion, will not be much influenced by either public opinion or the White House. But where there is enough market power, and hence enough discretion, for the guideposts to be a force, there is little or no reason to believe that the "free market" outcome will be in the public interest. The usual presumption against public interference in the market process does not hold. This conclusion does not depend on any very exact evaluation of the amount of competition to which the steel industry, or the aluminum industry, or the tobacco industry, or the United Automobile Workers, or the building trades unions are subject. It is enough that none of them is, and none of them thinks it is, selling against a nearly infinitely elastic demand curve.

Naturally, the fact that a concentrated industry and a strong union may make decisions not in the public interest does not automatically mean that what the guideposts suggest will be better. That question needs to be decided on its merits. Yet, the guideposts are intended to give a summary description of a well-functioning market economy; within limits they can be expected to represent the public interest fairly well. But it is much more important to realize that the public interest does need representation.

It is worth remembering, in this connection, that the guideposts are intended to have an effect on the general level of money wages and prices, not on relative wages and relative prices. Most of the things we expect free markets to accomplish are "real" things, more or less independent of the price level. Ideally, the guideposts should permit markets to allocate resources freely, insuring only that the price level not drift up in the process. The January 1962 Economic Report said: "It is desirable that labor and management should bargain explicitly about the distribution of the income of particular firms or industries. It is, however, undesirable that they should bargain implicitly about general price level." (P. 188.) In practice, one must admit, the guideposts will operate unevenly; relative prices and resource allocation may thus be affected. One can hope that these effects are second-order.

UNEVENNESS AND INEQUITY

This inevitable unevenness in operation strikes me as the main weakness in the guideposts. Public opinion is bound to have its greatest impact on markets that are centralized and conspicuous. That may not be all bad; centralization and discretionary power over prices and wages may be correlated. But there are obvious instances in which the correlation is broken, in which considerable market power in local markets goes along with decentralization and near-immunity to pressure from public opinion. The construction industry and the building trades unions are the standard illustration; parts of trade and transportation may provide other examples.

This weakness must simply be admitted. It is dangerous not only because it invites inefficient relative price effects, but because policy that tries to mobilize public opinion on behalf of the public interest will inevitably find its foundations sapped by obvious inequity.

There is probably no general solution to the problem. There may, however, be ad hoc solutions in special cases. If, as may well be the case, the Davis-Bacon Act is one of those legally enforced restrictions on competition whose main effect is to allow one segment of the labor market to exploit the others—and to hamper full-employment policy in the bargain—then repeal may well be in order.

Another possible solution to the problem of uneven impact might be to formalize the guideposts into some sort of advance-notice and/or public hearing procedure, perhaps through a committee of Congress. I am opposed to this sort of development. It would be a move away from the original conception of the guideposts as an educational device, in the direction of a system of semiformal price controls. It is unlikely that Congress would favor that much of a break with the past; if we are to espouse unlikely legislation, I would rather favor the promotion of competition and the reduction of tariff protection.

There is a different respect in which the involvement of Congress might be a good idea. Up to now, the burden of informing and mobilizing public opinion has fallen to the President and to the Chairman of the Council of Economic Advisers. This seems to be a mistake. The prestige of the President is probably too important a commodity to be spent in a way that invites occasional rebuff. And the prestige of the Council of Economic Advisers, taken by itself, is probably insufficient to carry the load. It might be helpful, therefore, if individual senators and congressmen would take part in the public debate, in their capacity as leaders and formers of public opinion. Even hearings are a possibility, provided they are hearings devoted to ordinary pieces of legislation—past or future—or to expert testimony and not to individual wage bargains or price decisions.

HOW SHOULD THE GUIDEPOST FIGURE BE SET?

In principle, the guidepost figure for wages is supposed to be the trend-increase in productivity for the economy as a whole. This is a difficult thing to measure; indeed, the concept is not entirely free of ambiguity. For example, one clearly wants a figure free of the effects of short-term changes in capacity utilization in industry, because otherwise the result would be to transfer the risks of enterprise from profits to wages, and that is not the intent. This suggests using a long-run trend figure. On the other hand, it seems faintly ridiculous that the permissible wage increase today should be made to depend on what was happening to productivity a few decades ago. Actually, this particular problem is primarily a matter of measurement, not of ambiguity in principle. A group of technicians could probably come to reasonable agreement. The difficulty is, however, that this number produced by technicians needs to be believed and used by the public and others. . . .

I am inclined to think that the technicians' methods should prevail. I realize that there are grave difficulties with this view. In the first place, the parties to collective bargaining are likely to resent being presented with a figure they had no part in setting. That is understandable. The trouble is that the parties' mutual relationship is naturally a bargaining one; presented with an opportunity to set or influence the guidepost figure, they will naturally bargain over it. But that would destroy any claim that the guidepost figure might have to be an objectively determined number. In the second place, I gather that some members of Congress would like to take a hand in guidepost-setting. Again, one can understand why. But in principle the guidepost figure is not something one sets, it is something that one finds out. Congress can investigate, of course, but it is far from clear that its methods are ideal for investigating the subtler properties of economic time series. I can imagine that every so often Congress might like to hear expert testimony on how the exercise is being carried out; that would be salutary. But that would be different from an airing of predictable majority, minority, and interested-party views.

There is another sort of problem which is not open to technical solution and on which exchanges of opinion might be useful. It was easy to begin talking about wage-price guideposts in 1962 because the immediate history was one of approximate price stability. But suppose prices have been rising, and suppose that it is very unlikely that they can be made to level out in one year. Then it is difficult for labor to acquiesce in a figure for money wage increases which would give the right real-wage increase only if prices were constant.

That would be to acquiesce to a subnormal increase in real wages and a supernormal increase in profits. On the other hand, to add the current rate of price increase to the rate of productivity increase would be to throw the entire burden onto profits or, more likely, guarantee that prices will continue to rise. What is needed is some target pace for slowing down the price trend over a couple of years. One can imagine rational discussion of such a problem in a small country with centralized and enlightened trade union and employer association leadership. (Even then I'm not sure one can imagine anything actually being accomplished on so difficult a matter.) It is less easy to imagine such discussion in the United States.

CONCLUSION

I have tried to convey the impression that wage-price guide-posts are not an ideal or complete policy for the control of inflation. They may, however, under appropriate circumstances, offer a little help at even less cost. Alternatives sometimes proposed may be very costly or very unrealistic. Let me quote an English author, Henry Smith (*Lloyd's Bank Review*, January, 1966, p. 40):

If the ideal answer is to allow the pricing system all the freedom that is possible, while creating an atmosphere which induces the maximum restraint on the use of strategic power capable of pushing up money wages and increasing prices, and this is probably the ideal solution, then out of the debate great good may come. If we go through the motions of working out what is called an incomes policy, although we cannot in reality put it into practice, then everybody on a position of strategic authorty may thnk twice before using it. This may not seem to be a great deal. However, the agreed objectives of British economic policy—rising productivity, expanding exports, economy in the use of manpower, high employment—all depend for their success upon the containment of the inflationary forces which their pursuit may generate.

Suggested Further Readings

Ashenfelter, Orley and George E. Johnson, "Bargaining Theory, Trade Unions, and Industrial Strike Activity," *American Economic Review,* March 1969.

Ashenfelter, Orley and Albert Rees, *Discrimination in Labor Markets* (Princeton University Press, 1973).

Bowen, William and T. Aldrich Finegan, *The Economics of Labor Force Participation* (Princeton University Press, 1969).

Burton, John and Charles Krider, "The Role and Consequences of Strikes by Public Employees," *Yale Law Journal,* January 1970.

Cain, Glen, *Married Women in the Labor Force* (University of Chicago Press, 1966).

Freeman, Richard, "Labor Market Discrimination: Analysis, Findings, and Problems," in M. Intriligator and D. Kendrick, eds., *Frontiers of Quantitative Economics* (American Elsevier Publishing Co., 1974).

Gwartney, James, "Discrimination and Income Differentials," *American Economic Review,* June 1970 and "Comment" by O. Ashenfelter and M. Taussig and "Reply" by Gwartney in the same journal, September 1971.

Hall, Robert E., "Why is the Unemployment Rate So High at Full Employment," *Brookings Papers on Economic Activity,* 1970:3.

Hamermesh, Daniel, ed., *Labor in the Public and Nonprofit Sectors* (Princeton University Press, 1975).

Holt, Charles, C. D. MacRae, S. O. Schweitzer, and R. E. Smith, *The Unemployment Inflation Dilemma: A Manpower Solution* (The Urban Institute, 1971).

Johnson, George E. and Frank Stafford, "The Earnings and Promotion of Women Faculty," *American Economic Review,* December 1974.

Kaufman, Jacob and Terry Foran, "The Minimum Wage and Poverty," in Sar Levitan, et. al., eds., *Towards Freedom from Want* (Industrial Relations Research Association, 1968).

Levitan, Sar, William Johnston, and Robert Taggert, *Still a Dream: The Changing Status of Blacks Since 1960* (Harvard University Press, 1975).

Lewis, H. Gregg, "Hours of Work and Hours of Leisure," *Proceedings of the Industrial Relations Research Association,* 1956.

————, *Unionism and Relative Wages in the United States* (University of Chicago Press, 1963).

Lovell, Michael, "The Minimum Wage, Teenage Unemployment, and the Business Cycle," *Western Economic Journal,* December 1972.

Ozanne, Robert, "Impact of Unions on Wage Levels and Income Distribution," *The Quarterly Journal of Economics,* May 1959.

Rees, Albert, *The Economics of Trade Unions* (University of Chicago Press, 1962).

Tobin, James, "Inflation and Unemployment," *American Economic Review*, March 1972.

Ulman, Lloyd and Robert Flanagan, *Wage Restraint: A Study of Incomes Policies in Western Europe* (University of California Press, 1971).

Welch, Finis, "Black/White Differences in Returns to Schooling," *American Economic Review*, December 1973.

——, "Minimum Wage Legislation in the U.S.," in Orley Ashenfelter, ed., *Evaluating the Labor Market Effects of Social Programs* (Industrial Relations Section, Princeton University, 1976).

Wellington, Harry and Ralph Winter, *The Unions and the Cities* (The Brookings Institution, 1971).

Wright, David McCord, ed., *The Impact of the Union* (Harcourt, Brace and World, 1951).

3